the resilient brand

STORYTELLING IN A DIGITAL ERA

Mahfuz Chowdhury

First Edition

eBook ISBN: 978-1-7750779-3-0
Hardback ISBN: 978-1-7750779-2-3
Paperback ISBN: 978-1-7750779-1-6

To my wife, who has been my rock throughout the long hours and late nights spent pouring over research and crafting the perfect sentences.

Your unwavering support and encouragement has been truly invaluable and a constant source of strength for me.

Your love and support has been the driving force behind the completion of this book and I am eternally grateful for all that you have done for me.

Thank you for being my partner in life and in this journey. I love you.

Contents

· · · · · · · · · ● ● ● · · · · · · · · · ·

introduction

Why Storytelling is the Future of Marketing, Like, Seriously.

· · · · · · · · ●● ● ●● · · · · · · · · · ·

Once upon a time, in a land far, far away, there was a powerful kingdom ruled by a wise and just king. The kingdom was known for its prosperity, and the people were happy and content. But one day, a great disaster struck. A fierce dragon appeared and began to ravage the land, destroying crops and homes, and terrorizing the people.

The king called upon his bravest knights to slay the dragon, but no matter how hard they tried, they could not defeat it. The dragon was too powerful and too clever. The people began to lose hope, and the kingdom began to fall into despair.

But the king knew that there was still one hope left. He called upon the kingdom's greatest storyteller, an old bard named Simon, who was known for his ability to weave tales that could inspire and uplift the spirits of the people.

Simon knew that the dragon was not just a physical threat, but also a psychological one. The dragon had instilled fear and hopelessness in the hearts of the people, and they had lost sight of the kingdom's strength and resilience. Simon knew that if he could change the people's perspective, they would be able to face the dragon with renewed courage and determination.

So, he began to tell stories of the kingdom's past heroes, who had faced and overcome great challenges. He told tales of their courage, their determination, and their unwavering belief in the kingdom's strength and resilience. He reminded the people of the kingdom's rich history and the many times they had overcome adversity.

As Simon's stories spread throughout the land, the people began to remember their own strength and resilience. They realized that they had the power to overcome the dragon, and they began to work together to defend their kingdom.

The dragon was eventually defeated, not by the sword of a knight, but by the power of storytelling. The kingdom was restored to its former glory, and the people lived happily ever after.

Storytelling is an art that can be used to build resilience and inspire action. Resilient brands use storytelling to remind their audience of their strength and capabilities, and to stay relevant in an ever-changing world.

When it comes to marketing, people are much more likely to remember and feel a connection to a brand if they can relate to the story behind it. It's not just about the numbers, it's about the emotional connection that storytelling creates.

That's why so many businesses today are using storytelling as a key part of their marketing strategy – because it works. It helps people feel a sense of community and familiarity with the brand, which is crucial for building loyalty and trust. But it's not just about building loyal customers – storytelling can also help your brand stay resilient in an ever-changing market.

By crafting authentic and engaging narratives that connect with your audience on an emotional level, you can differentiate your brand and establish a strong, **resilient identity** that stands the test of time.

I don't want to discount the importance of good research to back up the takeaways in this book, so let's start with the stats first:

> *According to a study by the Content Marketing Institute, brands that use storytelling in their marketing efforts see a 53% higher conversion rate compared to those that don't.*[1]
>
> *Another study by the Neuromarketing Science and Business Association found that storytelling activates the brain's emotional centers, making it more likely for consumers to remember and connect with a brand.*[2]

With these studies in mind, it's clear that storytelling is a powerful tool for businesses looking to build a strong and loyal customer base. As a business owner, marketer, or entrepreneur, you know that the world of marketing is constantly changing and evolving. So how do you keep up and make your brand stand out in a crowded market? The answer is by mastering **storytelling**.

By crafting authentic and engaging narratives that connect with your audience on an emotional level, you can differentiate your brand and build trust and credibility with your customers.

Storytelling is more than just a buzzword – it's the future of marketing, like, *seriously*. By crafting authentic and engaging narratives that connect with your audience on an emotional level, you can differentiate your brand and build trust and credibility with your customers.

But it's not just about telling a good story – it's about using storytelling to communicate the value of your brand and create a deeper connection with your audience.

Before we begin, it is crucial to consider the credibility of the source providing these insights. It's essential to understand the background and qualifications of the person delivering this information before putting it into practice and allowing it to influence your business decisions.

With that being said, please allow me to introduce myself:

As a Brand Storyteller with over a decade of experience, I have helped numerous businesses develop their unique narrative and create a story that resonates with their audience.

From small startups to global corporations, I have worked with a diverse range of brands and have acquired a comprehensive understanding of what it takes to craft a successful brand story.

Additionally, I am a highly sought-after speaker at international conferences, with a specialization in storytelling for brands. In other words, brand storytelling is one of the only few things in the world I'm a pro at. My goal is to assist you in constructing a strong and authentic brand narrative that will connect with your audience and differentiate you from the competition.

To be candid, I created this book mainly to help out some people I know. My intent is to give my wife a copy, which she can use to enhance her personal brand. And I wanted to pass it along to my team so they can have a guide to help them tell some killer stories. I even plan to keep a copy nearby for my own personal reference. In essence, I put all I've got into making this the only book needed to win at branding and storytelling.

This book is designed to provide practical guidance on how to harness the power of storytelling to benefit your business.

I'm not here to bore you with my personal stories (although I do have a separate book for that, should you be interested). We'll dive into the various ways that storytelling can help you build a resilient brand. From crafting epic customer stories to sharing your brand's origin story and values, we'll explore the various ways that storytelling can help you connect with your audience, foster a sense of community, and stand out in a crowded market.

With practical tips and examples from twenty of the world's most iconic brands, you'll learn how to use storytelling to create a strong and authentic brand narrative that will help your business thrive, now and in the future.

So if you want to build a brand that's resilient and ready to take on whatever challenges come your way, this book is for you.

So let's get started on crafting your brand's story and conquering the world (or at least your industry)!

chapter 1

The Art Of Storytelling
For Resilient Brands

· · · · · · ● · ● · · · · · · · ·

Once upon a time, in a far-off kingdom, there was a brand of shoes that was known for its durability and comfort. The shoes were made by a team of skilled cobblers who took great care in crafting each pair, but despite their quality, the brand struggled to survive in a market filled with flashier and trendier competitors.

One day, the head cobbler, a wise old dwarf named Ben, realized that the key to the brand's survival was in its storytelling. He understood that in order for the brand to be seen as resilient, it needed to communicate its values, heritage and the hard work that went into making every pair of shoes in a clear and consistent way.

Ben gathered his team and began to develop a strategy for storytelling that would focus on the brand's history, the unique craftsmanship and the dedication that went into making every pair of shoes. They began to share these stories through their website, social media, and local events. They also invited customers to share their own stories of how the shoes had lasted through different adventures and challenges.

As people heard the brand's stories, they began to see the shoes in a different light. They saw that the shoes were more than just a product, but a symbol of resilience, heritage and quality. They also began to see the brand as a responsible and trustworthy one that stood behind its products and its values.

Word of the brand's storytelling efforts spread quickly throughout the kingdom, and soon the brand became known for its resilience and durability. People were willing to pay more for the shoes because they felt like they were getting something special, and a product that would last for a long time. The brand's sales increased, and it was able to expand its business and create jobs in the community.

Are you tired of feeling like your brand is just another drop in the ocean of competition? Do you wish there was a way to truly stand out and make a lasting impression on your audience? It's time to break through the clutter!

As a business owner or marketer, you know firsthand how difficult it can be to cut through the noise and get noticed in today's crowded market. But storytelling is the key to breaking through and creating a genuine connection with your audience.

Think about it: when you hear a brand's origin story or customer story, it's much easier to feel a connection to them. It's not just about the facts and figures, it's about the emotional connection that storytelling creates.

That's why so many businesses today are using storytelling as a key part of their marketing strategy – because it works.

It helps people feel a sense of connection and familiarity with the brand, which can be incredibly powerful when it comes to building loyalty and trust.

But storytelling isn't just about building a loyal customer base. It's also about differentiating your brand in a crowded market.

By crafting a unique and compelling brand story, you can stand out from the competition and attract customers who are looking for something different. And in times of crisis or uncertainty, a strong brand identity can be a key factor in helping your business weather the storm.

By consistently communicating your brand's story and values, you can maintain a sense of stability and familiarity for your customers, even when other aspects of your business may be changing or uncertain.

It's time to embrace the power of storytelling. By crafting authentic and engaging narratives that connect with your audience on an emotional level, you can differentiate your brand, and build trust with your customers. It's time to become a resilient brand.

In this chapter, you'll learn how to use storytelling and take your business to the next level.

If you're looking to stand out in the digital age, storytelling is your secret weapon. It's about creating an emotional connection with your audience that will make you stand out from the competition. And the research backs it up.

According to Forbes, "Storytelling is the most powerful way to put ideas into the world today." And a study from the Wharton School of Business found that consumers are 22 times more likely to remember a message when it's delivered through a story, rather than just presenting the facts.[3, 4, 5]

Plus, research from the Center for Story-Based Strategy found that brands using storytelling in their marketing efforts can increase customer engagement by up to 50%.[6]

In other words, if you want to up your brand's game, it's time to start incorporating some killer storytelling into your marketing strategy.

GoPro

Adventure, Emotion, and Epic Storytelling

GoPro is a brand that has consistently utilized storytelling to connect with its audience and showcase its focus on adventure and action.

One highly effective campaign that demonstrates this is the "Be a Hero" campaign, which featured real people using GoPro products to capture their exciting and inspiring experiences.

The campaign featured real people using GoPro products to capture exciting and inspiring experiences, such as extreme sports, adventures in nature, and humanitarian work.

The campaign was highly effective in showcasing the versatility and durability of GoPro products, as well as the sense of thrill and accomplishment that can be captured with them.

By featuring real people and their personal stories, the campaign was able to create an emotional connection with its audience and inspire them to seek out their own adventures and experiences.

Through the use of compelling storytelling and high-quality video content, the "Be a Hero" campaign was able to effectively communicate GoPro's brand identity as a company that empowers people to capture and share their passions and achievements.

The campaign was successful in driving brand awareness and sales for GoPro, and has been credited with contributing to the company's success in the highly competitive action camera market.

Through sharing these authentic and engaging stories through visually stunning content, GoPro was able to not only highlight the capabilities of its products, but also create a sense of community and belonging among its customers.

This emotional connection, combined with GoPro's focus on adventure and action, has helped the company establish a strong brand identity and a dedicated customer base.

But the impact of GoPro's storytelling efforts goes beyond just promoting its products. By sharing these real, relatable stories, the company is able to create a deeper, more meaningful connection with its customers.

This not only helps to foster brand loyalty, but also allows GoPro to stand out in a crowded market.

GoPro's success with storytelling demonstrates the power of using authentic, engaging narratives to connect with and engage an audience.

Virgin

Brand Stories that Are Anything But Ordinary

Virgin is a company that has expertly used storytelling to establish itself as a leading brand in various industries.

The company's emphasis on innovation and disruption is integral to its brand story, which helps it stand out in a crowded market.

By sharing its values and mission through authentic and engaging narratives, Virgin has been able to create a strong brand identity that resonates with customers who value innovation and disruption.

One successful campaign that showcases Virgin's unique approach is the "Screw It, Let's Do It" campaign, launched in the early 2000s.

This campaign was launched in the early 2000s and was designed to showcase Virgin's unique and rebellious approach to business.

Through this campaign, Virgin sought to highlight their commitment to shaking up industries and challenging conventional wisdom.

To do this, they used storytelling to share stories about their unconventional business strategies and their willingness to take risks and embrace innovation.

This approach was highly effective in attracting customers who value disruption and are drawn to brands that are willing to challenge the status quo.

In addition to its focus on innovation and disruption, Virgin is also known for going above and beyond to create memorable experiences for their customers.

Whether it's through luxurious Virgin Atlantic flights or unique Virgin Hotels, the company is dedicated to providing exceptional experiences for its customers.

By sharing these stories through social media and other marketing channels, Virgin is able to create a sense of exclusivity and appeal to customers who are looking for something different.

Overall, Virgin's use of storytelling has been instrumental in helping the company establish a strong brand identity and differentiate itself in a crowded market.

Through its authentic and engaging narratives, Virgin has been able to create a deep connection with its customers and establish itself as a leading brand in multiple industries.

action guide

· · · · · · · · ● · · · · · · · · · · ·

With a newfound appreciation for the significance of storytelling, let's move on to practical steps for constructing a resilient brand:

Define your brand's story.

To define your brand's story, it is important to conduct thorough internal research to gain a deep understanding of your brand's mission, values, and unique selling points.

This research should be comprehensive and include reviewing all relevant company documents, as well as conducting interviews with key stakeholders such as founders, employees, and long-time customers. This will give you a clear understanding of what makes your brand unique and what its key messaging should be.

From this research, you should create a brand story document that outlines the key elements of your brand's story, including its mission, values, unique selling points, and key messaging. This document should serve as a guide for all of your storytelling efforts, and should be regularly reviewed and updated to ensure consistency across all of your branding and marketing efforts.

Highlight the unique features and benefits.

When crafting your stories, it is essential to highlight the unique features and benefits of your products and services. This will help to create a sense of excitement and desire among your audience, and differentiate your brand from your competitors.

Focus on the key customer benefits of your products and services, this will help you to create a sense of value for the customer and make them more likely to purchase.

Tap into emotions.

To tap into the emotions of your audience through storytelling, it is important to start by identifying the emotions that align with your brand and products.

For example, if your brand is all about wellness, you can tap into emotions such as relaxation, peace, and balance. This is essential because when your brand and products align with the emotions of your target audience, it will create a sense of connection and make them more likely to purchase.

Once you have identified the emotions that align with your brand, craft your stories in a way that evokes those emotions.

For example, you can share customer testimonials that show how your products or services helped them to relax, feel more peaceful, and achieve balance in their lives.

These stories will help to create an emotional connection with your audience and make them more likely to purchase from you.

Use emotional language and imagery in your stories to help your audience visualize and feel the emotions you're trying to evoke. This will make your stories more relatable and engaging and create a sense of connection with your audience.

Another way to tap into the emotions of your audience is to showcase the positive impact your products or services have on people's lives.

For example, if your brand sells eco-friendly products, you can share stories about how your products have helped to reduce pollution and have a positive impact on the environment. This way you are not only connecting with your audience on an emotional level, but also building trust and credibility for your brand.

Use storytelling across all channels.

To ensure that you are effectively using storytelling across all channels, it is important to first develop a comprehensive content strategy that outlines the types of stories you want to tell, the goals you hope to achieve, and the channels you will use to share them. This will help you to create a consistent brand voice and message and make sure that your audience is exposed to your stories regardless of where they come into contact with your brand.

To implement storytelling across different channels, you can take specific steps:

- Website: Incorporate storytelling elements into your website design, such as using imagery and language that evokes emotions and highlighting customer testimonials and case studies that showcase the value of your products and services.

- Social media: Use social media platforms to share behind-the-scenes stories, customer testimonials, and other engaging content that helps to build a deeper connection with your audience.

- Email marketing: Use storytelling in your email marketing campaigns to create a sense of urgency or excitement about your products and services.

- PR: Use storytelling to communicate your brand's messaging and values in press releases, interviews, and other PR materials.

By implementing storytelling across all channels, you will be able to create a consistent brand voice and message, increase the reach of your stories, and ensure that your audience is exposed to your stories regardless of where they come into contact with your brand.

Encourage customer engagement.

Encourage customer engagement by creating a platform where they can share their experiences and feedback with your brand, this can be done through a dedicated customer review section on your website, social media platforms, or through a customer survey. This will help you to gather valuable insights about your products and services and improve them based on customer feedback.

Make it easy for customers to share their stories and make sure to respond to their feedback in a timely manner. This will help to create a sense of connection and trust with your customers and make them more likely to engage with your brand.

Make sure to thank them for their feedback and take their feedback into consideration when making decisions about your products and services.

Use their stories in your marketing efforts and highlight the positive impact your products and services have had on their lives. This will not only create a sense of community among your audience, but also provide valuable insights that can be used to improve your products and services.

By highlighting customer stories, you can create a sense of trust and credibility with your audience, as they can see real-life examples of how your products and services have positively impacted others.

Use storytelling in product development.

Incorporating storytelling into the product development process can help to ensure that your products and services align with your brand's story and mission, this can be done by considering the story that each product tells.

Think about the emotions that the product evokes, such as how it can be used to improve people's lives, and how it can be used to solve a problem. This will help to make sure that the product you are creating is in line with your overall brand message and will resonate with your target audience.

Consider the benefits of your product from the customer's perspective, this will help to make sure that the product is valuable to your target audience.

Involving your target audience in the product development process by gathering feedback, can provide valuable insights and will help in creating products that align with the needs and wants of your customer. This can be done by conducting customer surveys, focus groups, and conducting interviews with your target audience. This will help to ensure that the product you are creating is aligned with the needs and wants of your target audience.

By involving your target audience in the product development process and creating products that align with your brand's story and mission, it will increase the chances of success when launching the product.

Measure the effectiveness of your storytelling.

To measure the effectiveness of your storytelling, it is important to set clear goals and objectives for your storytelling efforts, such as increasing website traffic or social media engagement. This will help you to determine if your storytelling efforts are achieving the desired results and make adjustments as needed.

Use web analytics tools to track the performance of your website and social media channels, and monitor metrics such as page views, bounce rate, and engagement. This will help you to see how your audience is interacting with your stories and make adjustments as needed.

Conduct customer satisfaction surveys to gather feedback on how your stories are resonating with your audience. Use this data to identify which elements of your storytelling are working well and which areas need improvement. This will help you to improve your storytelling efforts and make sure that they are resonating with your target audience.

Based on this analysis, adjust your storytelling strategy accordingly and continue to test and measure the results. This will help you to refine your storytelling approach and ensure that it is effectively driving business results.

Continuously update and refresh your stories.

In order to effectively keep your brand's stories relevant and interesting to your audience, it is important to continuously update and refresh them.

One way to achieve this is by regularly reflecting on new developments and changes within your industry or market and adapting your stories accordingly.

Utilize customer feedback, industry trends, and your own observations to update the elements of your stories.

It is crucial to ensure that your stories align with your brand's mission and values.

To keep your storytelling efforts fresh and engaging, encourage your team to come up with new ideas for stories that can be told about your products or services.

Consider experimenting with different types of content, such as videos, infographics, and social media posts, to keep your stories diverse and interesting, which will help to keep your audience engaged and coming back for more.

connecting the dots

· · · · · · · ●●●●●●●●●●● · · · ·

Now that we've discussed the importance of using storytelling to create a strong brand identity and connect with customers, it's time to dive into the art of telling epic customer stories.

These are the stories that showcase your brand through the eyes of your customers, highlighting their experiences and the impact your product or service has had on their lives. Telling these types of stories is a powerful way to showcase your brand's value and build trust with your audience.

In the next chapter, we'll explore how to craft and share customer stories that will captivate and inspire your audience.

chapter 2
Customer Stories: How to Tell Them and Why They Matter

· · · · · ●●●●● ● ●●●●● · · · · · ·

Once upon a time, in a magical kingdom, there was a small but ambitious shop that specialized in crafting unique and high-quality enchanted items. The shop was owned by a young fairy named Rose, who had a passion for magic and customer service. She had a team of skilled enchantresses who took great care in creating each enchanted item, but despite their hard work and dedication, the shop struggled to stand out in a crowded market.

One day, while visiting a trade show, Rose met a wise old wizard who shared a secret with her. He told her that the key to building a successful business was to tell the stories of her customers. "People want to know who they're buying from and how your enchanted items have made a difference in their lives," he said.

Rose took this advice to heart and began to collect stories from her customers. She asked them about their experiences with her enchanted items, the challenges they faced before finding her shop, and how the enchanted items had improved their lives. She listened to their stories with interest and empathy, and then shared them with her team, her online community and potential customers.

The stories resonated with people and they began to develop a strong emotional connection with the shop. They felt like they knew the shop and its team, and they trusted that they were buying enchanted items that were not only beautiful, but also made a difference in people's lives.

Word of the shop's unique and powerful customer stories spread quickly throughout the kingdom, and soon the shop became the go-to place for enchanted items. People were willing to pay more for Rose's enchanted items because they felt like they were getting something special. Her sales increased, and she was able to expand her business and create jobs in her community.

Are you ready to learn about how to use customer stories to take your brand to the next level? Because that's what we're diving into in this chapter. And let me tell you, it's a game changer.

Have you ever heard the saying "word of mouth is the best form of advertising"? It's true! When people hear about a brand from someone they know and trust, it carries a lot more weight than any ad or marketing campaign. That's where customer stories come in.

These stories showcase your brand through the eyes of your customers, highlighting their experiences and the impact your product or service has had on their lives.

Think about it – when you're considering making a purchase, don't you often look for reviews or testimonials from other customers? That's because hearing about a brand from a real person helps you feel more connected to it and builds trust. That's exactly what customer stories do.

By sharing these stories, you can showcase your brand's value and create a deeper connection with your audience. Plus, they're just really cool to read! Who doesn't love a good story?

As you've learned in Chapter 1, storytelling is a crucial element in building a successful brand. It allows you to connect with your audience in a meaningful way, differentiate yourself from the competition, and establish trust and credibility with your customers. But crafting an effective brand story isn't always easy. That's where Chapter 2 comes in.

In this chapter, you'll learn the art of telling epic customer stories, and how you can use them to not only engage your audience, but also drive sales and build brand loyalty.

Storytelling is the ultimate way to connect with your audience and turn them into loyal customers. It's more than just sharing information – it's about creating an emotional connection that resonates with your audience. And it's not just me saying it, the numbers back it up too.

> *According to Forbes, a massive 80% of consumers are more likely to make a purchase after hearing a brand's story. That's crazy, right?! But it doesn't stop there.[7]*
>
> *The New York Times conducted a study and found that customers who feel a personal connection to a brand are three times more likely to recommend it to others.[8]*

By sharing authentic and engaging customer stories, you can create a deeper connection with your audience, build trust and credibility, and ultimately drive sales and build brand loyalty.

Zappos

Winning Hearts Everywhere

Zappos is an online retailer that has leveraged storytelling to showcase its commitment to customer satisfaction.

The company is known for its excellent customer service, and has shared a number of customer stories on its website and social media channels to highlight the exceptional service its customers have received.

One notable example of this is the story of a customer was so pleased with the level of service she received from Zappos that she decided to express her gratitude in the form of a poem.

This poem, which has since been widely shared on social media and featured in various news articles, highlights the exceptional customer service that Zappos is known for and the lengths that the company goes to in order to ensure customer satisfaction.

The poem has been described as heartwarming and has likely helped to further strengthen the bond between Zappos and its customers.

Another example of Zappos' use of storytelling is the story of a customer who received a surprise delivery of flowers and a handwritten note from the company when she was feeling down.

This thoughtful gesture is just one example of the ways in which Zappos goes above and beyond for its customers and demonstrates its commitment to providing an exceptional customer experience.

By sharing this story and showcasing its commitment to going above and beyond for its customers, Zappos has likely been able to build trust and credibility with its audience and reinforce its brand identity as a company that values its customers.

Airbnb

Escaping Reality with Engaging Stories

Airbnb has effectively utilized storytelling as a key component of its marketing strategy, recognizing the power it has in connecting with customers and building trust and credibility.

To showcase the unique experiences of its hosts and guests, the company has a dedicated "Stories" section on its website that serves as a hub for personal stories.

Some stories are written articles that detail the experiences of hosts and guests, while others are videos that showcase the unique properties and experiences available on the platform.

These stories cover a wide range of topics, such as the cultural exchange that takes place between hosts and guests, the personal connections that are formed through Airbnb stays, and the unique and memorable experiences that are made possible through the platform.

By highlighting these stories, Airbnb is able to create an emotional connection with its audience and showcase the sense of community and belonging that are central to its brand identity.

This approach to storytelling helps to differentiate Airbnb from other vacation rental platforms and create a deeper level of engagement with its customers.

To effectively use storytelling in their marketing efforts, Airbnb focuses on real-life customer stories that showcase the emotional benefits of using their service. They use a variety of formats, including articles, videos, and podcasts, to share these stories and reach a wider audience.

In addition to their website, Airbnb also leverages social media to amplify and share these stories, helping to build trust and credibility with potential customers.

By sharing real, relatable stories, Airbnb has been able to create a deeper connection with its customers and establish itself as a leading player in the home-sharing industry.

action guide

· · · · · · ● ● ● ● ● ● ● ● ● ● · · · ·

Now that the importance of customer stories is clear, let's review some actionable strategies:

Identify your most satisfied customers.

To effectively identify your most satisfied customers, it is important to thoroughly review customer feedback, testimonials, and survey responses.

By analyzing this data, you can compile a list of customers who have had positive experiences with your brand and products or services.

Utilize this information to gain insight into the customer's needs and preferences, and to identify patterns and common themes that can inform your marketing and product development strategies.

Ask customers to share their story.

Once you have identified your most satisfied customers, reach out to them with a clear and detailed explanation of how their story will be used, such as being featured on your website or social media channels, and how it will benefit them. It is also important to obtain their consent before publishing their story.

Prepare a set of questions that will help you to gather all the information needed for their story, and make sure to provide them with a draft of the story before publishing it, to ensure that it accurately reflects their experience and that they are happy with how it is presented.

Showcase their experiences with your products or services.

To effectively create a customer case study or testimonial, it is important to first obtain the customer's permission to gather more information about their experience.

Conduct a detailed interview with the customer, asking about the specific challenges they faced before using your products or services and how your products or services helped them to overcome those challenges.

Make sure to include quotes from the customer and, if possible, include images to make the case study or testimonial more engaging and personal.

It's crucial to ask for feedback from the featured customer and ensure they are happy with the final outcome before publishing it.

Make the customer story more engaging and relatable.

To make customer stories more engaging and relatable, it is important to use storytelling techniques.

Start by setting the scene and describing the context and background of the customer's situation, introducing the customer as a relatable character and describing their problem or challenge.

Use a clear narrative structure to guide the audience through the story, highlighting the key points and building tension where appropriate.

Describe in detail how your products or services helped the customer to overcome this challenge and the positive outcome they achieved as a result.

This will help the audience to understand the value of your products or services and to see how they can be applied to similar situations.

Finally, conclude the story with a call to action that encourages the audience to take similar action or to contact you for more information.

Share the customer story across multiple channels.

To effectively communicate customer stories across all channels, it is important to utilize storytelling techniques on your website, social media, email marketing and PR. This will help to create a consistent brand voice and message and ensure that your audience is exposed to your stories regardless of where they come into contact with your brand.

Consider sharing customer stories on various platforms such as video content, podcasts, and in-person events. These platforms allow for a deeper level of engagement and reach a wider audience.

When sharing stories on different platforms, make sure to tailor the story to the specific platform and audience you're reaching out to. To maximize the impact, be strategic about when and where you share the customer story, considering factors such as the target audience and the timing of the campaign.

Encourage customers to share their stories.

To increase the reach and impact of your customer stories, it is important to make it easy for your customers to share their stories with their own networks. This can be achieved by including social sharing buttons on your website, such as those for Facebook, Twitter, LinkedIn, and Instagram. This will allow customers to easily share their stories with their own networks with a simple click.

You can create a referral program that rewards customers for sharing their positive experiences with your products or services. This can be done by offering a reward, such as a discount or a free product for every referral.

This approach will not only help to increase the reach of your customer stories but also create a sense of community and trust among your audience, as customers will be more likely to trust the recommendations of their friends and family.

Measure the results of your customer stories.

To measure the effectiveness of your customer stories, it is important to track engagement by monitoring likes, shares, comments, and views on your website and social media channels. This will give you an understanding of how well the customer stories are resonating with your audience.

Track sales and see if there is an increase in conversion rates or an increase in repeat customers, as this will indicate how effective the customer stories are in driving sales.

Track website traffic as well, to see if there is an increase in people visiting your website after the customer story has been shared.

Use this data to identify what is working well and what areas need improvement, and adjust your storytelling strategy accordingly. This will allow you to optimize your storytelling strategy and ensure that your customer stories are having the greatest impact possible.

Continuously gather customer feedback.

To continuously gather customer feedback, it is important to regularly conduct surveys by using tools like Google Forms, SurveyMonkey, or Typeform to gain insight into how customers feel about your brand and products.

Host focus groups or conduct customer interviews to gather qualitative data. This feedback can be used to improve your products and services, as well as your social media strategy and overall marketing efforts.

To ensure that your customers feel heard, it is also important to respond to customer feedback and comments on your social media platforms in a timely and professional manner. This shows your customers that you value their opinions and are dedicated to improving their experience with your brand.

Make sure to have a designated team member or team to monitor and respond to feedback, and establish a response protocol to ensure that feedback is handled efficiently and effectively.

Align your customer stories with your brand values.

It is crucial to ensure that your customer stories align with your brand values and messaging, and that they are consistent with the rest of your marketing efforts. This will help to ensure that your audience understands your brand's values and mission and how it aligns with the causes you support.

Consistency in messaging will help to ensure that your customers are able to identify with your brand and that it's easy for them to remember your brand.

To achieve this, you can start by conducting a thorough analysis of your brand's mission, values, and target audience. This will help you to identify the stories that are most relevant to your customers and align with your brand's mission and values.

Once identified, you can use these stories to create compelling customer stories that align with your brand values and messaging.

To ensure consistency, you can use the brand messaging guide you have developed earlier, to ensure that the customer stories align with your brand's key messaging points, tone, and style.

You can also use customer testimonials and statistics to further showcase the impact of your actions, providing evidence of how it has positively impacted the lives of your audience. This will help to ensure that your customer stories are consistent with the rest of your marketing efforts, making them more effective and impactful.

connecting the dots

Using storytelling to connect with your customers can be an effective way to build trust and credibility, differentiate your brand, and create a deeper emotional connection with your audience.

By sharing authentic and engaging customer stories, you can showcase the benefits of your product or service and build a strong brand identity.

Whether through social media, website content, or other marketing channels, using storytelling can be a powerful tool in your brand's marketing efforts.

chapter 3
Your Brand's Origin Story: More Than Just a Boring History Lesson

· · · · · ● ● ● ● ● ● ● ● ● ● ● · · · · ·

Once upon a time, in a land of myths and legends, there was a brand of potions and elixirs. The brand was created by a wise old wizard named Merlin, who had a deep understanding of magic and a passion for helping others. The potions and elixirs were made with rare and powerful ingredients, but despite their quality, the brand struggled to attract customers.

One day, Merlin realized that the key to the brand's success was in its origin story. He understood that in order for the brand to be seen as more than just a boring history lesson, he needed to communicate its values, heritage and the magic that went into making every potion and elixir in a clear, engaging and consistent way.

Merlin gathered his team and began to develop a strategy for storytelling that would focus on the brand's history, the unique ingredients and the magic that went into making every potion and elixir. They began to share these stories through their website, social media, and local events. They also invited customers to share their own stories of how the potions and elixirs had made a positive impact in their lives.

As people heard the brand's stories, they began to see the potions and elixirs in a different light. They saw that the potions and elixirs were more than just a product, but a symbol of magic, heritage, and tradition. They also began to see the brand as a responsible, trustworthy and magical one that stood behind its products and its values.

Word of the brand's storytelling efforts spread quickly throughout the land, and soon the brand became known for its magic and the positive impact it had on people's lives. People were willing to pay more for the potions and elixirs because they felt like they were getting something special, and a product that would make a positive impact in their lives. The brand's sales increased, and it was able to expand its business and create jobs in the community.

Okay, so if you haven't caught on by now, storytelling is basically the ultimate key to a successful brand. It allows you to create that all-important emotional connection with your audience, set yourself apart from the competition, and establish yourself as a trustworthy and credible business.

But let's be real, crafting an effective brand story isn't always easy peasy. That's where Chapter 3 comes in.

We're going to dive deep into the art of crafting a killer brand story that will not only captivate your audience, but also differentiate your brand and establish that trust and credibility we talked about.

In this chapter, we will dive into the importance of sharing your brand's origin story.

Your brand's origin story is more than just a boring history lesson – it's an opportunity to showcase your values, mission, and unique perspective on the world.

By sharing your brand's origin story in an authentic and engaging way, you can create a deeper connection with your customers and establish credibility and trust.

The power of storytelling to create an emotional connection with consumers cannot be overstated. Not only does sharing your brand's origin story allow you to showcase your values and purpose, it also helps to create a deeper level of engagement with your audience.

> *In fact, according to a study by Nielson, a staggering 72% of consumers said that they feel more connected to a brand when they understand its purpose and values.[9]*
>
> *But it's not just about building customer loyalty – a separate study by the University of California, Berkeley found that consumers are three times more likely to make a purchase from a brand that they feel an emotional connection to.[1011]*

So if you want to drive sales and build brand loyalty, sharing your brand's origin story is a must!

Many businesses today are using their origin stories as a way to connect with their customers and stand out in a crowded marketplace.

Ben & Jerry's

A Scoop Of Social And Environmental Justice

Founded in 1978 by Ben Cohen and Jerry Greenfield, Ben & Jerry's started as a small ice cream shop in Vermont.

The company quickly gained a following for their unique flavors, such as Chunky Monkey and Cherry Garcia, and their commitment to using all natural ingredients. However, it wasn't just their delicious ice cream that helped Ben & Jerry's stand out.

In the 1980s, Ben & Jerry's made the decision to use their business as a platform for social and environmental change.

They became the first ice cream company to label their products as fair trade, demonstrating their commitment to ethical business practices.

They also established the Ben & Jerry's Foundation, which supports grassroots organizations working towards social and environmental justice.

In addition to using their business to promote social and environmental causes, Ben & Jerry's has also consistently used storytelling to communicate their values and mission to their customers.

By sharing their origin story and values with their customers, Ben & Jerry's has been able to build a strong and loyal customer base that is drawn to the company's commitment to making a positive impact on the world.

Today, Ben & Jerry's is still known for their delicious ice cream, but they are also recognized for their commitment to using business as a force for good.

Whether through their fair trade practices, their support of grassroots organizations, or their commitment to sustainability, Ben & Jerry's has consistently demonstrated their values through their actions and used storytelling to share their message with their customers.

Nike

A Scoop Of Social And Environmental Justice

Nike's origin story has played a significant role in the company's marketing efforts since the company's early days.

The famous "Just Do It" campaign, which was launched in the late 1980s, was a major turning point for the company.

The campaign featured the story of how Nike co-founders Phil Knight and Bill Bowerman started the company, and how their vision of creating high-quality athletic shoes and gear was born.

Through this campaign, Nike was able to tap into the emotional needs of its target audience – athletes – and inspire them to push themselves to their limits and "Just Do It."

The "Just Do It" campaign was highly successful, and it helped to cement Nike's position as a leader in the athletic industry.

The campaign was iconic and it is still remembered today as one of the most successful and memorable advertising campaigns in history. It helped to create a strong and cohesive brand identity for Nike, and it also helped to establish the company as a trusted and reliable source of athletic footwear and apparel.

By sharing the story of how the company was founded and its core values, Nike was able to create an emotional connection with its customers and inspire them to be their best selves.

But Nike's commitment to storytelling extends beyond just their origin story. The company has also made a dedication to corporate social responsibility and sustainability, and this commitment is rooted in the company's origins.

Knight and Bowerman were both passionate about using their business to make a positive impact on the world, and this commitment to using business as a force for good is reflected in Nike's numerous sustainability initiatives.

Nike's sustainability efforts have been a major focus for the company in recent years. As part of their commitment to sustainability, Nike has set a goal to become carbon neutral by 2030. This ambitious goal involves reducing the company's carbon emissions and offsetting any remaining emissions through investments in renewable energy and other carbon reduction projects.

In addition to their efforts to reduce their carbon footprint, Nike has also made significant strides in reducing waste and water usage in their supply chain. For example, the company has implemented programs to recycle materials and water in their manufacturing processes, and they have worked with their suppliers to adopt more sustainable practices.

By consistently communicating their sustainability efforts to their customers and stakeholders, Nike has been able to showcase their commitment to sustainability and differentiate themselves in the crowded athletic industry.

By sharing their origin story and values, Nike has been able to create a deeper connection with their customers and differentiate themselves from competitors.

action guide

· · · · · · ●●●●●●●●●●● · · · · · · ·

Having grasped the crucial nature of your brand's origin story, let's turn our attention to some concrete steps:

Identify the key elements of your origin story.

To create an authentic and engaging brand story, it is important to first reflect on the key elements that make up the origin of your brand. This includes delving into the background of how the company was founded, highlighting any major milestones or turning points that have occurred throughout the company's history, and identifying the values and mission that guide the brand's decisions and actions. This information will serve as the foundation for all of your storytelling efforts and will help you to create a story that accurately represents your brand.

Once you have a clear understanding of the key elements of your brand's origin story, it is crucial to research and gather any additional information and details that will help to bring that story to life. This can include conducting market research to understand your target audience and the types of stories that resonate with them, as well as researching the industry and competitors to understand the larger context in which your brand operates.

With a clear and complete understanding of your brand's origin story, you can then begin to craft your stories in a way that will connect with your audience on an emotional level and create a sense of purpose and meaning that inspires loyalty and drives business results. This may include creating a brand narrative that aligns with your target audience's values and interests, and using storytelling techniques such as emotional storytelling, storytelling through customer testimonials, and visual storytelling to engage your audience and create a deeper connection with your brand.

Develop an engaging and authentic narrative.

To develop a narrative around your brand's origin story, it's essential to start by identifying the key elements that make up the foundation of your brand. This could include the background of the company's founding, any major milestones or turning points, and the values and mission that drive the brand.

Once you've identified these key elements, it's important to think about how they can be woven together to create a cohesive story that is both engaging and authentic to your brand.

To make the story more engaging and relatable, it's vital to highlight the emotional connection that your brand has with its customers and how it aims to make a positive impact in the world. This will help to create a sense of purpose and meaning that resonates with your audience, and inspires loyalty towards your brand.

To make your brand story more engaging and impactful, you can use storytelling techniques such as setting the scene, creating a character and using a clear narrative structure.

It is important to make sure that the story is consistent with your brand's messaging and values across all marketing channels. This can be achieved by incorporating the brand story into all marketing efforts, such as website, social media, email marketing and other brand communications.

Share your origin story across multiple channels.

When sharing your brand's origin story, it's essential to ensure consistency in the tone and message across all channels. This will help to create a sense of familiarity and trust with your audience, as they will be able to recognize and relate to your brand's story no matter where they come across it.

To achieve consistency, you can create a brand style guide that outlines the tone, messaging, and language to be used across all marketing efforts.

To make your brand story more engaging and reach a wider audience, it's important to consider using different formats to share your story. This could include creating a company history page on your website, producing a video series on social media platforms, or creating an infographic that visually communicates your brand's origin story.

You can also use events or press releases to share your origin story with a wider audience and generate media coverage. This can help you reach new audiences and create brand awareness.

Incorporate your origin story into your marketing efforts.

To effectively incorporate your brand's origin story into your branding and marketing efforts, it's important to first identify the key elements that make up the foundation of your brand. This includes the background of the company's founding, any major milestones or turning points, and the values and mission that drive the brand.

Once you've identified these key elements, you can then develop a narrative around them that is both engaging and authentic to your brand.

The narrative should focus on highlighting the emotional connection that your brand has with its customers, and how it aims to make a positive impact in the world.

By emphasizing on the emotional aspect and purpose of your brand, it will help to create a sense of connection and loyalty with your audience.

Once the narrative is developed, it's important to share it across multiple channels to reach a wider audience. This can include creating a dedicated company history page on your website, sharing video content on social media platforms, and incorporating the story in other marketing materials like brochures, email campaigns, and presentations.

You can also use events or press releases to share your origin story with a wider audience and generate media coverage.

Create a special landing page dedicated to your origin story.

To effectively create a dedicated landing page on your website to showcase your brand's origin story, it's important to first develop a clear and compelling narrative of your brand's origin story. This includes highlighting the background of the company's founding, any major milestones or turning points, and the values and mission that drive the brand.

Once you have developed this narrative, you can then create a dedicated landing page on your website that prominently features this story.

It's important to use engaging visuals and storytelling techniques on this page to make it both informative and engaging for visitors. This could include using images, videos, infographics and other design elements that help to bring the story to life.

Including calls to action on the page such as signing up for a newsletter or following your social media accounts, it can help to encourage visitors to engage with your brand further and deepen their connection to your brand.

By creating a dedicated landing page on your website, you can ensure that your audience is exposed to your origin story and can understand the meaning and purpose behind your brand, which can ultimately drive loyalty and business results.

connecting the dots

Now that we've explored the importance of sharing your brand's origin story in building a strong and authentic brand identity, it's time to focus on how to use storytelling to showcase your products.

Product storytelling can be a powerful way to differentiate your offering and create an emotional connection with your customers.

In the next chapter, we'll dive into the art of crafting compelling product stories that will wow your customers and drive sales.

chapter 4

Product Stories That Will Wow Your Customers

· · · · · · · · ● ● ● ● ● ● · · · · · · ·

Once upon a time, in a kingdom of wonders, there was a brand of jewelry that specialized in creating unique and beautiful pieces. The brand was owned by a young and talented fairy named Aurora, who had a passion for art and storytelling. The jewelry was crafted with great care, using only the finest materials, but despite its beauty, the brand struggled to attract customers.

One day, Aurora realized that the key to the brand's success was in the stories behind each piece of jewelry. She understood that in order for the brand to stand out, she needed to communicate the inspiration, the history and the artistry that went into creating every piece of jewelry in a clear, engaging and consistent way.

Aurora gathered her team and began to develop a strategy for storytelling that would focus on the stories behind each piece of jewelry. They began to share these stories through their website, social media, and local events. They also invited customers to share their own stories of how the jewelry had made a positive impact in their lives.

As people heard the brand's stories, they began to see the jewelry in a different light. They saw that the jewelry was more than just a product, but a symbol of art, history, and creativity. They also began to see the brand as a responsible, trustworthy and artistic one that stood behind its products and its values.

Word of the brand's storytelling efforts spread quickly throughout the kingdom, and soon the brand became known for its unique and beautiful jewelry. People were willing to pay more for the jewelry because they felt like they were getting something special, a piece of art with a story. The brand's sales increased, and it was able to expand its business and create jobs in the community.

Are you ready to learn how to take your product marketing to the next level with storytelling? Because let me tell you, it's not just about listing off features and specs – it's about creating a narrative that showcases the unique benefits of your product and how it can enhance your customers' lives. And trust me, people are much more likely to remember and be persuaded by a product story that resonates with them emotionally.

So get ready to learn how to craft product stories that will not only impress your customers, but also drive those all-important sales.

By crafting compelling and engaging narratives that showcase the unique features and benefits of your products, you can create a deeper connection with your customers and increase the perceived value of your products.

In this chapter, we'll explore the art of crafting product stories that will wow your customers and drive sales.

Research shows that storytelling can have a seriously positive impact on consumer perception of your brand.

In fact, a study by Forbes found that 77% of consumers have a more positive outlook on a brand after reading a custom content piece that includes storytelling.[12]

And it's not just consumers who are on board with the power of storytelling – a survey conducted by the Content Marketing Institute revealed that a whopping 73% of companies believe that storytelling is a crucial part of their content marketing strategy.[13]

So, if you want to differentiate your brand in the market and drive sales, learning how to craft compelling product stories is a must.

Apple

Thinking Different With Personalization

· · · · · · ●●●● ● ●●●● · · · · · ·

Apple has a long history of using storytelling to create compelling product narratives and establish a strong brand identity. One key way that the company has done this is through the use of emotional marketing and personalization in their advertising campaigns.

For instance, the "Shot on iPhone" campaign featured real-life photos taken by iPhone users, highlighting the high-quality camera and advanced technology of the device. From breathtaking landscapes to intimate portraits, the "Shot on iPhone" campaign demonstrated the versatility and high-quality of the iPhone camera.

By showcasing the work of everyday iPhone users, the campaign was able to create a sense of authenticity and relatability, making it more relatable and appealing to its target audience.

Additionally, the campaign was highly successful in driving brand awareness and sales, making it a prime example of the power of storytelling in marketing.

In addition to emphasizing the user experience in their product storytelling, Apple has also consistently highlighted the social and environmental responsibility of their products.

For instance, Apple has long emphasized the sustainability of their products, including their use of recycled materials and energy-efficient manufacturing processes.

They have also highlighted the accessibility features of their products, such as VoiceOver, which allows users with visual impairments to interact with their devices.

Additionally, Apple has used their platform to raise awareness about social and environmental issues, such as climate change and education, and has donated proceeds from certain products to charitable organizations

By consistently incorporating these themes into their product storytelling, Apple has been able to communicate their values and mission to their customers and build a strong and authentic brand identity.

But Apple's use of storytelling doesn't just stop there. The company has also used storytelling as a way to engage with their customers and build a sense of community around their brand.

For example, Apple has a number of programs and initiatives that encourage customers to share their stories and experiences with the company's products.

These programs provide a platform for customers to share their stories and connect with others who share similar interests, helping to create a sense of community and belonging around the Apple brand.

Overall, Apple's use of storytelling has been instrumental in helping the company establish a strong brand identity and differentiate itself in the highly competitive tech industry.

Tesla

Storytelling at the Speed of Innovation

TAKE A
NEW ROAD

ROADSTER 2.5 →

Tesla, an electric vehicle company, has long recognized the power of storytelling in marketing their brand and has implemented this strategy across various platforms.

From visually stunning product launch events to compelling social media campaigns, Tesla has effectively used storytelling to create a strong and loyal customer base.

One example of this is Tesla's "The Roadster" campaign, which was launched to promote the company's new electric sports car.

The campaign featured a series of videos that highlighted the sleek design, advanced technology, and impressive performance of the Roadster.

Through compelling visuals and engaging narratives, Tesla was able to create a sense of excitement and anticipation among potential customers and showcase the unique selling points of their product.

In addition to highlighting the technical capabilities of the Roadster, the campaign also focused on the environmental benefits of electric vehicles and how they contribute to a more sustainable future.

By weaving this message into their storytelling, Tesla was able to appeal to a wider audience and communicate their values and mission as a company.

Overall, the "The Roadster" campaign was highly effective in helping Tesla showcase the unique features and benefits of their product and create a strong emotional connection with their target audience.

In addition to showcasing the features and benefits of their products, Tesla has also used storytelling to emphasize their commitment to sustainability and innovation.

The company often shares stories about the environmental impact of their electric vehicles and the ways in which they are pushing the boundaries of technology.

This emphasis on sustainability and innovation is central to Tesla's brand identity and is reflected in their product offerings and business practices.

For example, Tesla has made a commitment to using sustainable materials in their products and minimizing waste in their supply chain. They have also implemented a number of initiatives to reduce their carbon footprint, such as transitioning to renewable energy sources for their manufacturing processes.

Furthermore, Tesla has a strong focus on innovation and is known for their cutting-edge technology and advanced features.

From self-driving capabilities to advanced safety features, Tesla has consistently pushed the boundaries of what is possible in the automotive industry.

action guide

· · · · · · ●●●● ● ●●●● · · · · ·

As you now comprehend the value of great product stories, let's proceed to specific tactics for strengthening your story:

Identify the unique features and benefits of your products.

Before you begin to craft compelling stories that effectively highlight the value of your products, it is crucial to take the time to deeply understand the key features and benefits that set your products apart from those of your competitors. This may include elements such as superior quality, innovative design, or exclusive features that are not offered by other brands.

One way to uncover this information is to conduct market research, such as surveying current customers or conducting focus groups with potential target audiences, to gain a better understanding of what they look for in products similar to yours.

Once you have a clear understanding of what makes your products unique, you can use this information to craft stories that effectively showcase their value to your audience. This could involve highlighting real-life examples of how your products have helped customers solve specific problems, or emphasizing the unique features and benefits of your products in a way that speaks to the needs and desires of your target audience.

By understanding what makes your products unique, you can use this information to target specific customer groups who are most likely to be interested in these features and benefits.

For example, if your products have a unique feature that appeals to a specific demographic, such as eco-conscious consumers, you can tailor your marketing efforts to reach and engage this group.

Tell a story.

Instead of simply listing the features and benefits of your products, use storytelling to create a narrative around them that helps your audience to envision themselves using your products and see how they can improve their lives.

To create a clear and compelling narrative, start by setting the scene and introducing a character that your audience can relate to, who faces a specific problem or challenge.

For example, you could introduce a busy working mother who struggles to find time to cook healthy meals for her family.

Next, show how your product or service helps to solve that problem and the positive impact it has on the character's life. Use descriptive language, imagery, and anecdotes to bring the story to life and make it more relatable and engaging for your audience.

For example, you could describe how the busy working mother uses your meal delivery service to easily and quickly prepare healthy meals for her family, saving her time and stress.

Consider using video or other visual content to help bring the story to life in an even more engaging way.

For example, you could create a video that shows the busy working mother using your meal delivery service, as well as the happy reactions of her family as they enjoy the meals together. This can help to create a more immersive and emotional connection with your audience.

Use visuals.

To help create a sense of excitement and desire among your audience, use high-quality images and videos to showcase your products in action. This can include photographs of your products being used in real-life scenarios, such as a customer using your skincare products or cooking with your kitchen appliances, as well as videos that demonstrate the features and benefits of your products.

For example, you could create a video that shows how easy it is to set up and use your new electronic device, or how a certain feature of your product can make a task easier.

Consider using product animations or interactive elements to help your audience better understand and engage with your products.

For example, you can create an animation that shows the inner workings of your product, or an interactive feature that allows customers to virtually customize or try on your product.

To ensure that your visuals accurately represent your products and are visually appealing, be sure to use high-quality images and videos that are well-lit, in focus, and professionally edited. It's also important to ensure that the visuals are properly sized and optimized for different platforms, such as social media, website or email marketing.

Create a sense of scarcity.

To create a sense of urgency around your products and encourage your audience to take action and make a purchase, use storytelling to emphasize the limited availability or exclusivity of your offerings. This can be achieved by highlighting the limited stock of your products, and emphasizing the time-sensitive nature of any discounts or promotions you may be offering.

For example, you could create a sense of scarcity by announcing that your products are available for a limited time only, or that you have a limited number of units available for purchase. This could include a countdown timer on your website, or a message that indicates how many units are left in stock.

You could also use language and imagery that emphasizes the exclusivity of your products, such as emphasizing that your products are only available to a select group of customers, or that they are the first to have access to a new product or limited edition.

To make your story more relatable and engaging for your audience, you can use real-life examples of how your products have helped customers solve specific problems, or emphasizing the unique features and benefits of your products in a way that speaks to the needs and desires of your target audience.

It's also important to be consistent in your storytelling throughout all your marketing channels, whether it's an email, website, social media, or in-store. This will help create a cohesive message and increase the chances of your audience taking action.

Use customer testimonials.

To add credibility to your product stories and create social proof, reach out to satisfied customers and ask them to provide a testimonial about their experience with your products or services.

To ensure that you have a diverse range of testimonials that showcase the range of benefits your products can provide, make sure to collect testimonials from a variety of customers, such as different age groups, genders, and occupations.

When collecting testimonials, you can use various methods such as sending out a survey to your customer base, reaching out to them directly through email or phone, or by using a third-party tool that specializes in collecting customer reviews.

Once you have collected testimonials, incorporate them into your product stories. This could include adding them to your website, social media accounts, email marketing campaigns, or in-store displays.

To make the testimonials more relatable and trustworthy, use customers' names and photos, when possible. This will help your audience to visualize real people who have had positive experiences with your products and services, which can make them more likely to trust your claims and consider purchasing your products.

You can also use video testimonials for a more personal and engaging touch. Make sure to ask permission from the customer if you want to use their video and if they are comfortable with it.

Use emotional appeal.

To tap into the emotions of your audience and create a sense of desire and motivation to purchase your products, use storytelling to highlight how your products can help improve their lives. This can be achieved by focusing on the specific benefits and value that your products provide, and how they can help to solve a problem or improve the customer's life in some way.

One effective way to do this is by creating a story about a customer who was able to achieve a specific goal or overcome a specific challenge thanks to your product.

For example, you could tell the story of a busy working mother who was able to find more time for herself and her family thanks to your time-saving kitchen appliance. This will help your audience to envision themselves in a similar situation and see how your product can improve their lives.

To make the story more relatable and engaging, you can use descriptive language, imagery, and anecdotes to bring the story to life.

Also, consider using real-life examples of how your products have helped customers solve specific problems, or emphasizing the unique features and benefits of your products in a way that speaks to the needs and desires of your target audience.

It's also important to make sure your story is consistent with your brand message and values and that it aligns with your target audience. This will help create a stronger emotional connection with your audience and increase the chances of them taking action.

Use humor.

To make your product stories more engaging and memorable, use storytelling to incorporate humor by using witty puns, clever wordplay, or relatable scenarios that make your audience laugh and connect with your product on a deeper level.

To ensure that your humor aligns with your brand's tone of voice and message, consider hiring a copywriter or a creative team who can help you come up with ideas that are both funny and appropriate for your brand.

Before using your humorous ideas in your marketing campaigns, it's important to test them in a focus group or with a small sample of your target audience to see if it resonates with them and make adjustments accordingly. This will help you to fine-tune your humor to ensure it will be well-received by your target audience.

Always keep in mind that humor should not be offensive or in bad taste and it should always align with your brand's values. It's important to make sure that your humor is respectful and inclusive, and that it doesn't offend or alienate any of your target audience.

Also, it is important to use humor in moderation, not all stories should be humorous, and it should be used strategically and thoughtfully.

Humor can be an effective tool to connect with your audience, but it should not detract from the main message of your story or the benefits of your product.

Create a sense of mystery.

To create a sense of mystery around your products through storytelling, one way is to hint at the unique features or benefits of your products without revealing too much information. This can be done through the use of clever headlines, intriguing taglines, or teaser videos that showcase the product in a mysterious or unexpected way.

For example, you could use a tagline such as "Unlock the secret to better skin" or create a teaser video that shows the product in action but doesn't reveal the brand name or specific details.

Another way to create a sense of mystery is by announcing the launch of a new product or service and providing only a limited amount of information about it. This can create a sense of anticipation and excitement among your audience, encouraging them to stay engaged with your brand and look forward to the launch. You can use social media, email marketing or in-store displays to announce the launch and share sneak peeks of the product.

You can also create a sense of mystery by sharing a story about a customer who has achieved great success with your product, but keeping the identity of the customer anonymous. This will keep the audience guessing and increase their interest in your product. You can also use testimonials that are anonymous or use testimonials that are not fully disclosed, this will make the audience curious to know more about the product.

· · · · · · ●●●● ● ●●●●● · · · · ·

connecting the dots

· · · · · · ●●●● ● ●●●●● · · · · ·

Now that we've explored the importance of sharing your brand's origin story in building a strong and authentic brand identity, it's time to focus on how to use storytelling to showcase your products.

Product storytelling can be a powerful way to differentiate your offering and create an emotional connection with your customers.

In the next chapter, we'll dive into the art of crafting compelling product stories that will wow your customers and drive sales.

chapter 5

Staying on Brand:
The Importance of Consistency
in Storytelling

· · · · · ● ● ● ● ● ● ● ● ● ● ● · · · ·

Once upon a time, in a land of magic and wonder, there was a brand of enchanted candles. The candles were crafted by a team of skilled sorcerers who took great care in selecting the finest ingredients and creating a variety of enchantments. The candles were a hit with customers, and the brand quickly became known for its high-quality and unique products.

As the brand grew, the sorcerers began to experiment with new enchantments and designs, and they started to tell different stories about their candles. They began to create new characters and different enchantments for different product lines, and as a result, their messaging and branding became inconsistent.

The customers were confused by the inconsistent branding and messaging, and they no longer felt a connection to the brand. Sales began to decline, and the sorcerers didn't understand why.

One day, a wise old sorcerer named Carina visited the brand and noticed the inconsistencies in their messaging and branding. She explained to the sorcerers that staying consistent with their branding and messaging was crucial for building a connection with their customers and making them feel like they were buying something special.

The sorcerers took Carina's advice to heart and began to focus on telling consistent stories about their candles and their brand. They went back to their roots and focused on the enchantments that had made their candles so special in the first place. They also began to use consistent characters and messaging across all their product lines.

As customers saw the consistent branding and messaging, they began to feel a connection to the brand once again. Sales increased, and the brand was able to regain its reputation for high-quality and unique enchanted candles.

Have you ever stopped to think about how important consistency is when it comes to telling your brand's story?

I mean, think about it – if your brand's messaging and values are all over the place, how are customers supposed to know what you stand for and what they can expect from you? That's where the importance of consistency in storytelling comes into play.

When you consistently communicate your brand's message and values through all of your marketing efforts, you create a cohesive and believable brand narrative that your audience can trust and feel connected to. And in today's competitive market, building that trust and connection with your customers is crucial for standing out and driving sales.

So, if you want to crush your brand game and create a loyal customer base, make sure to keep consistency in mind when crafting your brand's story.

By using storytelling to stay on brand and convey a consistent message, you can create a strong and cohesive brand identity that resonates with your audience.

In this chapter, we'll explore the importance of consistency in storytelling and how you can use it to create a strong and memorable brand.

It's no secret that consistency is key when it comes to building a successful brand.

When it comes to storytelling and branding, being consistent helps establish trust and credibility with your audience and creates a strong and memorable brand identity. And let's be real, who doesn't want that for their business?

According to a study by Forbes, consumers are much more likely to trust and be loyal to brands that have a consistent message and identity. But it's not just about creating trust and loyalty with your customers - being consistent in your branding can also increase brand recognition and recall. [14]

In fact, research by the Huffington Post found that consistent branding can lead to a whopping 23% increase in revenue. Talk about the power of consistency! [15]

But it's not just about being consistent in your branding - a survey by the Content Marketing Institute found that consistent messaging was the second most important factor in a successful content marketing strategy, with only "relevant and valuable" content ranking higher.

By staying consistent in your storytelling and branding efforts, you can create a strong and memorable brand identity that resonates with your audience and drives business success.

So, if you want to take your brand to the next level, it's time to focus on consistency.

Starbucks

Consistently Comforting

WE SERVE THE BEST COFFEE IN THE WORLD.
NOW YOU CAN SERVE IT TOO

BRING HOME THE STARBUCKS COFFEE MAK
available now at Starb

From marketing campaigns to store design, Starbucks has carefully crafted its brand identity and consistently delivered a high-quality customer experience.

One way that Starbucks has consistently communicated its brand message is through its marketing campaigns.

For example, the company's "Coffee at Home" campaign, which Starbucks launched in the early 2010s, was designed to showcase the versatility of the company's products and highlight the ways in which they can be enjoyed in the comfort of one's own home.

To achieve this, Starbucks created a series of advertisements that featured customers using Starbucks coffee, tea, and other products in various domestic settings, including in the kitchen, living room, and bedroom.

The ads featured a range of images, including close-ups of steaming mugs of coffee, people enjoying their drinks while lounging on the couch, and even people enjoying Starbucks products in bed.

Accompanying each image was a tagline that reinforced the idea that Starbucks is a place to relax and unwind, such as "Coffee at home. It's the perfect way to end the day" and "Coffee at home. It's where the magic happens."

Through this campaign, Starbucks was able to effectively communicate its brand message and create an emotional connection with its audience.

Similarly, the company's "Meet Me at Starbucks" campaign, which highlights the role that Starbucks plays as a social gathering place.

This campaign features real customers sharing their personal stories and experiences of meeting friends and loved ones at Starbucks, and emphasizes the sense of community and connection that is central to Starbucks' brand identity.

Through authentic and relatable storytelling, this campaign effectively creates an emotional connection with its audience and showcases the unique role that Starbucks plays in people's lives.

These stories about people coming together and enjoying each other's company at Starbucks creates a sense of community and belonging among its customers.

In addition to its marketing efforts, Starbucks has also maintained a consistent brand identity through its store design.

From the cozy seating areas to the warm color palette, Starbucks stores are designed to create a welcoming and inviting atmosphere. This consistency in store design helps to reinforce the brand message and create a sense of familiarity for customers.

Finally, Starbucks has consistently delivered a high-quality customer experience.

From the friendly baristas to the wide variety of food and drink options, Starbucks has created a customer experience that is in line with its brand message.

This attention to detail and commitment to customer satisfaction has played a key role in the company's success and helped to build a loyal customer base.

This is a key takeaway for any brand looking to use storytelling to build a successful and enduring brand.

By consistently communicating its brand message and delivering a high-quality customer experience, a company can create a strong brand identity and establish a loyal customer base.

· · · · · · ● · · · · · · · · · ·

Lego

Creating Memories One Brick At A Time

· · · · · · ● · · · · · · · · · ·

Lego has consistently used storytelling as a key part of its branding and marketing efforts, recognizing the power it has in engaging with its customers and communicating its brand identity.

Through its marketing campaigns, themed sets, and corporate social responsibility efforts, Lego has consistently emphasized the values of creativity, imagination, sustainability, and education.

One of the most notable examples of Lego's use of storytelling is its "Build with Us" campaign, which features a series of stories that showcase the transformative power of building with Lego.

These stories illustrate how building with Lego helps children (and adults) develop important skills such as problem-solving, creativity, and spatial awareness.

By sharing these stories, Lego is able to showcase the benefits of its products and create an emotional connection with its audience.

In addition to featuring stories about the benefits of building with Lego, the "Build with Us" campaign also includes a variety of interactive and immersive experiences, such as Lego building challenges and workshops, that encourage people of all ages to get hands-on with Lego and discover the joy of building.

Overall, the "Build with Us" campaign is a powerful example of how Lego has used storytelling to connect with its audience and promote the benefits of its products.

In addition to its marketing campaigns, Lego has also used storytelling to showcase its commitment to sustainability and education through its partnership with the United Nations.

Through this partnership, Lego has supported various initiatives aimed at promoting sustainability and education, such as providing access to clean water and building schools in underserved communities.

As social media has become an increasingly important platform for brands to share their stories, Lego has also leveraged the power of social media to connect with its audience and share its brand's story in a compelling and authentic way.

From crafting engaging posts to collaborating with influencers, Lego has used social media to deepen its connection with its customers and build a loyal following.

action guide

In light of your understanding of the importance of consistency, let's explore practical measures for building a resilient brand:

Define your brand's unique voice and message.

In order to define your brand's unique voice and message, it is essential to first identify the key elements that differentiate your brand from others in the market. These elements may include your brand's mission statement, core values, and unique selling points that set you apart from competitors.

Once these key elements have been identified, it is important to create a set of guidelines that outline the tone, language, and overall messaging you wish to convey to your target audience. This should include specific elements such as the tone you want to use, the types of words and phrases you want to use, and the types of stories you want to tell in order to connect with your audience.

Once you have defined your brand's unique voice and message, it is crucial to implement it consistently across all marketing efforts, including your website, social media, email marketing, and public relations. This will help to establish a sense of familiarity and trust with your audience, while also ensuring that your message is communicated clearly and effectively.

Create guidelines for your brand's voice and message.

To ensure consistency in your brand's voice and message, it's important to develop a set of guidelines that clearly outline the tone, language, and overall messaging you want to convey to your target audience. These guidelines should be shared with all team members, to ensure that everyone is on the same page when it comes to the messaging and tone of the brand.

Additionally, it is important to include examples of the types of content that should align with these guidelines, such as social media posts, website copy, email campaigns, and more. This will provide a clear understanding of what type of content aligns with your brand's voice and message.

To ensure consistency, all brand-related content should be reviewed against these guidelines as a reference, and any necessary adjustments should be made to align it with your defined brand voice and message.

Consistency in your brand image will help to create trust with your audience over time.

Train your team members on how to use the guidelines effectively.

To ensure that everyone on your team is familiar with and understands the guidelines for your brand's voice and message, it is important to provide training sessions that explain the guidelines in detail and provide examples of how they should be applied in different types of content. This can be done through group training sessions, one-on-one coaching, or providing written or video resources.

Additionally, it's important to establish a regular review process where you check the work of your team members to ensure consistency in their application of the guidelines and make any necessary adjustments. This review process could be on a weekly, bi-weekly or monthly basis, depending on the size of your team and the volume of content being produced.

It's important to also establish a clear feedback system so that team members can ask questions and receive guidance on how to improve their adherence to the brand's guidelines.

Regularly review your brand's voice and message.

To ensure consistency in your brand's voice and message across all channels, it is important to conduct regular audits of your brand's content such as social media posts, website copy, email campaigns, and more. This can be done by reviewing each type of content and looking for any inconsistencies in the tone, language, and messaging, and making any necessary adjustments.

To further ensure that your brand's voice and message resonates with your target audience, consider gathering feedback from your customers through surveys, focus groups, or by monitoring social media comments. This feedback can provide valuable insights into how your audience perceives your brand's voice and message, and help you identify areas for improvement.

You can also conduct market research to understand how your brand's voice and message is resonating with your target audience compared to competitors. This will help you make any necessary adjustments to your brand's voice and message to ensure that it remains consistent, effective and relevant over time.

Track the performance of your content.

To effectively track the performance of your content and identify areas where you need to improve consistency in your brand's voice and message, it is important to use analytics tools to measure key metrics such as engagement rates, website traffic, and conversion rates. This data can provide valuable insights into how your audience is interacting with your content and help you identify any inconsistencies in your messaging.

To effectively use analytics, it's important to set up tracking on your website and social media platforms, and regularly review the data to identify trends and make any necessary adjustments to your brand's voice and message.

To gain a deeper understanding of how your audience perceives your brand, consider conducting surveys or focus groups to gather feedback from your audience. This feedback can provide valuable insights into how well your brand's voice and message resonates with your target audience, which can help you make more informed decisions about how to improve consistency in your brand's voice and message.

Use customer feedback to improve your brand's message.

To ensure that you are effectively communicating your brand's unique voice and message, it is important to encourage customer feedback and use it to improve your brand's message.

One way to do this is by conducting surveys and sending them to your customers, asking them to rate their experience and provide feedback on the overall messaging and communication of your brand.

Another way is to host focus groups with a diverse group of customers to gain a deeper understanding of how they perceive your brand, and what they think could be improved. You can also conduct customer interviews to gain more in-depth insights into their experiences and perceptions of your brand, and use this information to inform your messaging and improve consistency across all channels.

By regularly gathering customer feedback and using it to improve your brand's message, you can ensure that you are effectively connecting with your audience and building strong relationships with them.

Continually adapt your brand's voice and message as your business evolves.

To ensure that your brand's voice and message stays relevant and effective, it is important to continually adapt them as your business evolves. This means regularly reviewing and updating your messaging to ensure that it aligns with your current target audience and goals.

One specific action step to take is to conduct market research to understand the current needs and wants of your target audience.

It is also important to keep an eye on industry trends and adapt your messaging accordingly.

Furthermore, it is also important to gather customer feedback and use it to improve your brand's message by conducting surveys, hosting focus groups or conducting customer interviews to gain insight into how your customers perceive your brand and what they want to see from you in the future.

Finally, ensure that your messaging is consistent across all channels and platforms.

· · · · · · · · · ● · · · · · · · · · · ·

connecting the dots

· · · · · · · · · ● · · · · · · · · · · ·

As the digital age has progressed, social media has become an increasingly important platform for brands to tell their stories.

In Chapter 6, we'll explore the ways in which businesses can use social media to engage with their audience and share their brand's story in a compelling and authentic way.

From crafting engaging posts to leveraging the power of influencer marketing, there are numerous ways in which businesses can use social media to connect with their audience and share their brand's story.

Whether you're just starting out on social media or looking to take your efforts to the next level, this chapter will provide valuable insights and tips for using social media to tell your brand's story.

chapter 6
#StorytellingGoals: How to Use Social Media to Tell Your Brand's Story

· · · · · · · · · ● · · · · · · · · · · ·

Once upon a time, in a kingdom of magic and wonder, there was a brand of enchanted potions. The potions were crafted by a team of skilled sorcerers who took great care in selecting the finest ingredients and creating a variety of powerful enchantments. The potions were a hit with customers, but the brand struggled to reach new audiences and increase its visibility.

One day, a wise old sorcerer named Milo, who was an expert in the art of magic, visited the brand and noticed their struggles. He explained to the sorcerers that in the modern world, one of the most powerful ways to reach new audiences and increase visibility was through the use of social media.

The sorcerers were skeptical at first, but they decided to give it a try. They created a social media strategy that focused on telling the story of their brand and their enchanted potions. They shared pictures and videos of the ingredients they used, the enchantments they created, and the positive impact their potions had on people's lives.

As they began to share their story on social media, they quickly noticed an increase in engagement and followers. People were captivated by the story of the brand and its enchanted potions, and they were eager to learn more.

The sorcerers also used social media to connect with their customers and listen to their feedback. They used this feedback to improve their potions and create new enchantments that their customers would love.

Word of the brand's enchanting potions and their story began to spread throughout the kingdom, and soon the brand became known for its powerful and unique enchanted potions. The brand's sales increased, and it was able to reach new audiences and expand its business

If you're a business owner or marketer looking to make an impact on social media, you're in the right chapter. We're going to dive into the ways you can use social media to tell your brand's story and connect with your audience.

We all know that social media is constantly evolving, and it can be tough to keep up. But by using storytelling to create authentic and engaging content, you can stand out in the sea of marketing messages and make a real impact on social media.

Chapter 6 explores the various ways in which brands can leverage social media to tell their stories and engage with their audience.

From crafting compelling visuals and content to using hashtags and user-generated content, there are many strategies that brands can use to effectively tell their stories on social media.

In this chapter, we'll dive into the key considerations for using social media for storytelling.

Social media is a game-changer when it comes to brand storytelling. Not only does it allow businesses to connect with their audience in real-time, but it also provides the opportunity to create a two-way conversation and encourage customer engagement. And let's face it, we all love a good story!

According to a study by Forbes, social media users are more likely to remember and share a brand's story if it's presented in a visually appealing and engaging way.[16]

Plus, by using hashtags and user-generated content, businesses can amplify their brand's story and reach an even wider audience. It's no wonder that 81% of small and medium businesses use social media to promote their business, with 3.6 billion social media users worldwide.[17]

Zara

From The Runway To Your Instagram Feed

Zara, a fashion retailer known for its sleek and trendy clothing, has effectively used storytelling through its social media presence to differentiate itself from competitors and create a loyal following.

Zara has consistently used visually stunning content to engage with its customers and showcase its products.

The company's Instagram account is a prime example of this, as they use professional photographers and models to create high-quality and visually appealing posts.

By using this approach, Zara is able to capture the attention of their audience and create a sense of excitement and anticipation around their products.

In addition to using professional photographers and models, Zara also incorporates a wide range of creative elements into their Instagram content, such as eye-catching graphics, bold colors, and unique styling.

These creative elements help to differentiate Zara's content from other fashion brands and keep their audience engaged and interested.

Additionally, the high-quality images and carefully curated content on the company's Instagram account helps to reinforce the luxury and sophistication of their brand.

By consistently sharing visually appealing and creatively crafted posts, Zara has been able to engage with its audience and showcase its products in a unique and memorable way.

In addition to showcasing their products through visually stunning posts, Zara also uses Instagram Stories to give their followers a behind-the-scenes look at the creative process, from designing new pieces to shooting campaigns. This provides a more authentic and engaging experience for their followers and helps to build a stronger connection with their audience.

By sharing these glimpses into their brand's inner workings, Zara is able to showcase the care and attention that goes into creating their products and create a sense of transparency and trust with their customers.

But it's not just about the visuals – Zara also uses their social media platforms to share their brand values and mission with their followers. They regularly post about sustainability initiatives and partnerships, emphasizing their commitment to environmental and social responsibility.

By consistently incorporating these themes into their storytelling, Zara has been able to establish a deeper connection with their audience and further differentiate themselves in the competitive fashion industry.

Honest Tea

Sipping On Sustainability

Honest Tea is a company that has consistently used social media to tell its brand story and engage with its customers.

From showcasing the personal and meaningful experiences offered by its products and services, to highlighting its commitment to sustainability and social responsibility, Honest Tea has effectively used social media to create powerful and memorable experiences for its audience.

One key way that Honest Tea has used social media to connect with its customers is by highlighting the personal and meaningful experiences that its products and services offer.

Whether through sharing customer reviews or showcasing the ways in which its products fit into everyday life, Honest Tea has effectively used social media to create a deeper connection with its audience.

In addition to showcasing the personal experiences offered by its products and services, Honest Tea has also consistently used social media to highlight its commitment to sustainability and social responsibility. From sharing stories about its sustainability initiatives to promoting its partnerships with organizations that align with its values, Honest Tea has effectively used social media to communicate its brand values and mission.

Overall, Honest Tea's use of social media has been instrumental in helping the company build a strong and cohesive brand identity. By consistently sharing authentic and engaging content that showcases its products, values, and commitment to sustainability and social responsibility, Honest Tea has been able to create meaningful connections with its customers and drive brand advocacy.

action guide

· · · · · · · · ●●● ● ●●● · · · · · ·

Now that you grasp the significance of using social media, let's discuss actionable methods for sharing your story:

Develop a social media strategy.

Developing a social media strategy that focuses on engaging and authentic content can be an effective way to build a strong online presence and connect with your target audience.

One specific action step is to conduct a social media audit to understand the current performance of your social media accounts, analyze your audience, and identify the best platforms to reach your target audience.

Another step can be to create a content calendar that includes a mix of different types of content (e.g. educational, entertaining, promotional) that aligns with your brand's voice and messaging.

You can also use analytics tools such as Facebook Insights, Twitter Analytics and Google Analytics to track the performance of your content and make data-driven decisions on what types of content are resonating with your audience.

To make sure that your content is engaging and authentic, you can use a variety of formats such as text, images, videos, infographics, live streaming and polls. Furthermore, you can incorporate user-generated content, and collaborate with influencers, industry experts and thought leaders to create a sense of trust and authenticity among your audience.

Highlight the unique features and benefits of your products and services.

Using storytelling to create a narrative around the unique features and benefits of your products and services can help your audience envision themselves using them and see how they can improve their lives.

To do this, you can share real-life examples of customers using your products through customer testimonials, case studies, and photos or videos that showcase the products in action. This will help create a sense of excitement and desire among your audience.

One specific action step is to conduct customer interviews and collect their feedback, testimonials, and photos or videos of them using the product. You can use this material to create a case study that highlights the benefits of the product and how it has improved their lives.

You can also create a video series featuring customer testimonials, and share them on your social media platforms and website.

Furthermore, you can use these customer stories to generate social proof and create a sense of trust and authenticity among your audience.

Share your brand's origin story.

Sharing your brand's origin story and values can be an effective way to connect with customers on an emotional level.

To do this, you can highlight the founding of the company, any major milestones or turning points, and the values and mission that drive the brand. This information can be shared through various social media platforms such as Instagram, Facebook, Twitter, and LinkedIn.

You can also use storytelling techniques to make the origin story more engaging by including personal anecdotes and highlighting the emotional connection that your brand has with its customers.

Furthermore, it's important to show how your brand is making a positive impact in the world and the causes it supports. This can be done by creating content that highlights your brand's involvement in community projects, charitable initiatives, and sustainability efforts.

By doing so, you can create a sense of purpose and meaning among your audience, and help them connect with your brand on a deeper level. This can be shared through different platforms such as corporate social responsibility blog, social media post, video and infographics.

Listen to customer feedback.

Have a system in place to actively listen to customer feedback. One way to do this is by setting up notifications for mentions of your brand on various social media platforms, such as Twitter, Instagram, and Facebook. This will allow you to stay informed of any comments or messages related to your brand in real-time.

Furthermore, actively engaging with customers by responding to their comments and messages shows that you value their feedback and are dedicated to improving their experience with your brand.

To take it a step further, you should use the feedback to identify areas where your products or services can be improved. This can be done by conducting regular customer satisfaction surveys, performing data analysis on customer feedback and complaints, and monitoring social media mentions for common themes or issues.

Once you have identified areas for improvement, you can then make adjustments accordingly. This could include updating product features, revising service processes, providing additional customer support, or improving the overall customer experience.

In order to ensure that changes are effective, it's important to track the progress of your actions and measure the impact on customer satisfaction.

Track engagement and reach.

Regularly monitor and analyze the engagement and reach of your storytelling content on social media. This can be done by utilizing social media analytics tools, such as those provided by the individual platforms (such as Facebook Insights or Instagram Analytics) or third-party tools like Hootsuite or Sprout Social.

By tracking metrics such as likes, shares, comments, and click-throughs, you can gain a better understanding of which types of content are resonating with your audience and which are not.

Based on this data, you can then adjust your strategy accordingly by creating more of the content that is performing well and less of the content that is not.

You can use this data to identify key demographics, such as age and gender, that are most engaged with your content and tailor your messaging to better reach those groups.

Create a consistent brand voice and message.

Establish a consistent brand voice and message across all your social media platforms. This can be achieved by developing a brand style guide that outlines the tone, language, and messaging that should be used on each platform.

This guide should also include guidelines for visual elements such as logo placement, color palette and typography.

Once the style guide has been developed, it should be shared with all team members who will be creating and managing content for your social media platforms.

In addition, it is important to regularly review and update the guide to ensure that it remains relevant and consistent with your overall brand strategy. This consistency will help in creating a sense of familiarity and trust with your audience.

Another way to achieve consistency is by creating a content calendar, where you plan and schedule your posts in advance, this will help you align the message and voice of your brand across all platforms and make sure that the themes and topics you cover are consistent with your overall brand strategy.

Showcase your corporate social responsibility and sustainability efforts.

Use social media to showcase your corporate social responsibility and sustainability efforts. This can be done by creating dedicated social media content that highlights the specific actions your company is taking to make a positive impact on society and the environment. This could include posts about charitable initiatives, community engagement, and environmental conservation efforts.

You can use social media to share stories of the people and communities you are impacting through your efforts, which can help to create a deeper sense of purpose and meaning for your audience.

To create a sense of purpose and meaning that inspires loyalty and drives business results, it is important to be transparent and authentic in your messaging.

Use social media platforms to share data and metrics that demonstrate the impact of your efforts. You can also create social media campaigns that encourage your audience to get involved and make a difference themselves. This can help to create a sense of community and shared purpose among your followers.

Another way to create a sense of purpose is by using social media to share your company's values and mission statement. This will help to create a deeper connection between the brand and the audience, and will make them more likely to be loyal customers.

Lastly, it is important to track and measure the success of your social media campaigns related to corporate social responsibility and sustainability. This can be done by monitoring metrics such as engagement, reach, and sentiment to understand how your audience is responding to your efforts. Use this data to optimize your campaigns and ensure that they are having the desired impact.

Engage with your audience.

Actively engage with your audience on social media by responding to comments, starting conversations, and encouraging user-generated content. This can be done by regularly monitoring your social media accounts for comments and messages, and responding promptly and respectfully. This will show your audience that you value their input and are actively listening to their feedback.

To start conversations, you can use social media polls, quizzes, and questions to encourage your audience to share their thoughts and opinions. This can help to create a sense of community among your followers and increase their engagement with your brand.

Encouraging user-generated content is another way to increase engagement and create a deeper connection with your followers. This can be done by running social media contests or campaigns that incentivize your audience to share their own content featuring your brand. This type of content is often more authentic and relatable, which can help to increase trust in your brand.

It is also important to track the success of your engagement efforts by monitoring metrics such as engagement rate, click-throughs and retention rate. Use this data to optimize your engagement strategy and ensure that it is having the desired impact.

Iit is also important to recognize and appreciate your audience's contributions, by featuring their content on your social media platforms, sending them thank you messages or even offering rewards, this will make them feel valued and more likely to continue to engage with your brand.

Offer exclusive promotions, deals, and discounts.

It is important to use social media to offer exclusive promotions, deals, and discounts to your followers. This can be done by creating unique coupon codes or promotional codes that can only be redeemed through your social media platforms. This creates a sense of exclusivity and encourages your followers to engage with your brand more frequently.

You can use social media to announce flash sales or limited-time offers. This creates a sense of urgency and encourages your followers to act quickly to take advantage of the deal.

Another way to increase loyalty and drive business results is by creating social media-exclusive loyalty programs. This could include rewards for sharing your brand's content, referring friends, or making purchases through your social media platforms.

To track the success of your promotions and deals, you can use social media analytics tools to monitor metrics such as click-throughs, engagement rate, and conversion rate. This data can help you understand which promotions are resonating with your audience and which are not.

It is also important to use A/B testing to see which promotions works best, this could mean testing different types of promotions (e.g. discounts, buy one get one free, etc.) and different messaging to see which ones get the best results.

Lastly, it is important to communicate your promotions clearly and effectively, by using eye-catching graphics, clear and direct call-to-action and making sure your promotions are easily redeemable, this will increase the chances of your followers taking advantage of the offers and drive business results.

Create compelling and engaging content.

It is important to use storytelling to create compelling and engaging content that resonates with your audience and adds value to their lives. To do this, you can start by identifying the unique stories, values and experiences that are specific to your brand. Use these to create content that aligns with your brand's message and mission.

Another way to create compelling stories is by highlighting the people behind your brand, such as employees, customers, or partners. Sharing their personal experiences and perspectives can help to create a more relatable and authentic connection with your audience.

You can also use storytelling to create educational and informative content that provides value to your audience. This could include how-to guides, case studies, and expert advice. By providing helpful information, you can position your brand as a valuable resource and establish trust with your audience.

To create engaging content, it is important to use a variety of formats and media such as videos, images, infographics and animation, this will make your content more visually appealing and increase the chances of it being shared and engaged with.

It is also important to track and measure the success of your storytelling content by monitoring metrics such as engagement rate, click-throughs, and retention rate. Use this data to optimize your content strategy and ensure that it is resonating with your audience.

Lastly, it is important to be consistent with your storytelling, by creating and sharing content on a regular basis and using similar themes and formats, this will help to build a narrative and create a deeper connection with your audience.

connecting the dots

By understanding the needs and desires of your audience and crafting authentic and engaging stories that tap into those emotions, you can use social media to tell your brand's story and drive business results.

Now that you've learned how to use social media to effectively tell your brand's story, it's time to explore how to incorporate storytelling into your content marketing strategy.

In Chapter 7, we'll dive into the world of content marketing and how you can use storytelling to create valuable, informative, and engaging content that aligns with your brand's values and mission. By crafting compelling stories that resonate with your target audience, you can drive profitable customer action and establish trust and credibility with your customers.

chapter 7

The Lowdown on Using Storytelling for Epic Content Marketing

· · · · · · · · ● · · · · · · · · · ·

Once upon a time, in a kingdom of myths and legends, there was a brand of magical swords. The swords were crafted by a team of skilled blacksmiths who took great care in selecting the finest materials and creating a variety of powerful enchantments. The swords were a hit with customers, but the brand struggled to reach new audiences and increase its visibility.

One day, a wise old sorcerer named Gandalf visited the brand and noticed their struggles. He explained to the blacksmiths that in order to reach new audiences and increase visibility, they needed to focus on creating epic content that would capture people's attention and imagination. He suggested they use storytelling as a way to showcase the power and uniqueness of their swords.

The blacksmiths were intrigued by Gandalf's idea and decided to give it a try. They created a content marketing strategy that focused on telling the stories of their swords, the enchantments they held and the heroes that wielded them. They created videos, blog posts, and social media content that showcased the swords in action, and how they helped the heroes in their quest.

As they began to share their stories, the brand's visibility increased and they began to reach new audiences. People were captivated by the stories of the swords and the heroes that wielded them, and they were eager to learn more.

The blacksmiths also used their content to connect with their customers and listen to their feedback. They used this feedback to improve their swords and create new enchantments that their customers would love.

Word of the brand's powerful and unique swords and their epic stories began to spread throughout the kingdom, and soon the brand became known for its exceptional swords. The brand's sales increased as more and more people wanted to own a piece of the magic and adventure they had read or seen in the stories. The brand's reputation grew as well, as people associated the swords with bravery, strength and the sense of adventure.

The blacksmiths also found that the storytelling approach helped them in building strong relationships with their audience and customers. They were able to create a deeper connection with them and make them feel like they were part of the story and the adventure.

Have you ever heard the saying "content is king"? Well, it's especially true when it comes to using storytelling to connect with your customers and build a successful brand.

In today's digital age, consumers are constantly bombarded with an endless stream of marketing messages, so it's more important than ever to stand out and differentiate your brand. And one of the best ways to do this is through content marketing.

By crafting valuable, informative, and engaging content that aligns with your brand's values and mission, you can attract and retain a clearly defined audience and ultimately drive profitable customer action.

But let's be real, creating content that stands out in a crowded market is no easy feat. That's where storytelling comes in. By incorporating storytelling into your content marketing strategy, you can create an emotional connection with your audience and make your brand's message more memorable and impactful.

Think about it – when you read a customer story or brand origin story that resonates with you, you're much more likely to feel a connection to that brand and be more likely to make a purchase.

In recent years, content marketing has become a buzzword in the marketing world, and for good reason. By creating valuable and informative content that aligns with a brand's values and mission, businesses can attract and retain a clearly defined audience, ultimately driving profitable customer action. And one of the most effective ways to do this is by incorporating storytelling into your content marketing strategy.

In this chapter, we will dive into the world of content marketing and explore how storytelling can be used to create epic content that engages and inspires your audience.

Storytelling is a powerful tool in content marketing, with 91% of B2B marketers and 86% of B2C marketers using it as part of their marketing strategy.

It's no surprise that it's so popular – a study by the Demand Gen Report found that 70% of B2B buyers prefer to learn about new products and services through articles rather than advertisements.[18]

This shows just how effective storytelling can be in engaging and educating customers in a more authentic and relatable way.

It's a great way to build trust and credibility, as well as establish a deeper connection with your audience.

So if you're not already using storytelling in your content marketing efforts, it's definitely worth considering – you could see some amazing results!

Red Bull

Soaring To New Heights With Stunning Storytelling

Red Bull is an energy drink brand that has consistently used storytelling to build a strong and cohesive brand identity.

The company is known for its creative and visually stunning advertising campaigns that often involve extreme sports, adventure, and entertainment.

One of the company's most iconic campaigns is the "Red Bull Gives You Wings" slogan.

Launched in the late 1990s, the campaign used the slogan as a metaphor for the energy and boost that the drink provides.

The campaign featured a variety of creative and eye-catching ads that depicted people doing extreme and adrenaline-fueled activities, such as skydiving, snowboarding, and motocross.

These ads effectively conveyed the brand's message of providing energy and excitement to its target audience of thrill-seekers and adventurers.

In addition to traditional print and television ads, the campaign also included experiential marketing elements such as sponsored events and competitions, as well as a strong presence on social media. Through these various channels, Red Bull was able to reach a wide audience and create a strong brand identity that is still recognized and remembered today.

One key way that Red Bull has incorporated storytelling into its content marketing strategy is through its Red Bull Media House, a content production company that creates and distributes high-quality video and written content about extreme sports, adventure, and entertainment.

From sponsoring record-breaking stunts to producing award-winning documentaries and original series, Red Bull Media House has made storytelling a central part of its marketing efforts.

Red Bull Media House has also produced a wide range of high-quality video and written content that tells the stories of the athletes, adventurers, and entertainers who embody the brand's values and mission.

By consistently sharing exciting and visually stunning content that resonates with its target audience of thrill-seekers and adventurers, Red Bull has been able to create a strong brand identity and differentiate itself in the crowded energy drink market.

Marriott

Where Every Stay Is A Story Worth Telling

················●············

Marriott is a company that has consistently used storytelling to engage with its customers and communicate its brand identity.

Through campaigns like "Travel Brilliantly," Marriott aimed to showcase the unique experiences offered by Marriott hotels to travelers.

The campaign featured real stories of travelers and the memorable experiences they had while staying at Marriott hotels. These stories were shared through a variety of mediums, such as social media, online articles, and video content.

The goal of the campaign was to create a personal and authentic connection with Marriott's audience and highlight the company's commitment to providing exceptional travel experiences.

To achieve this, the campaign focused on storytelling, using real-life examples to illustrate the unique experiences offered by Marriott hotels.

But Marriott's use of storytelling doesn't stop at its marketing efforts. The company has consistently emphasized the high-quality customer experience offered by its hotels, from luxurious amenities to exceptional service.

This focus on customer experience is reflected in the company's numerous awards and accolades, and has helped to further strengthen its brand identity.

In addition to its customer experience, Marriott has also used storytelling to highlight its commitment to sustainability and social responsibility.

The company has implemented various initiatives to reduce its environmental impact and give back to the communities in which it operates.

By consistently incorporating these themes into its storytelling, Marriott has been able to demonstrate its values and mission to its audience.

action guide

························●···········

As you are now aware of the magnitude of content marketing, let's proceed to some practical steps:

Align with your target audience's interests and emotions.

Identify key elements of your brand's story that align with your target audience's interests and emotions. This can be done by conducting market research and gathering data on your target audience's demographics, behaviors, and preferences. Use this information to understand their needs and values, and identify the elements of your brand's story that align with them.

Once you have identified these key elements, you can use them to create a content strategy that resonates with your audience. This can include creating social media campaigns, blog posts, videos, infographics and other types of content that highlight these elements and align with your target audience's interests.

To ensure your content is resonating with your audience, you can use A/B testing to experiment with different formats, messages, and visuals, and measure which ones are getting the best results.

Track and measure the success of your content by monitoring metrics such as engagement rate, click-throughs, and conversion rate. Use this data to optimize your content strategy and ensure that it is resonating with your audience.

It is important to be consistent with your messaging and storytelling, by creating and sharing content on a regular basis and using similar themes and formats, this will help to build a narrative and create a deeper connection with your audience.

Lastly, it is also important to be authentic and transparent, by being true to your brand's values and mission and creating content that is relatable and valuable to your target audience, this will help to establish trust and credibility with your audience.

Create a variety of content formats.

Diversify the types of content you create in order to reach a wider audience and effectively communicate the value of your products and services.

One strategy to consider is to incorporate customer testimonials, case studies, behind-the-scenes looks, and product demos into your content mix.

For example, you could create a series of blog posts that feature customer success stories and highlight the specific ways in which your products and services have helped them.

Produce video content that gives a behind-the-scenes look at your company and showcases the people and processes that make your products and services possible.

You could also create infographics that break down complex ideas or data related to your products and services in an easy-to-digest way.

Finally, consider creating social media posts that highlight key features and benefits of your products and services, and include product demos to give potential customers a better understanding of how they can be used.

Create a consistent narrative across all of your content.

One effective way to create a deeper connection with your audience and increase brand recall is to use storytelling throughout all of your content.

To start, you should establish a consistent narrative that aligns with your brand's mission and values.

This narrative should be woven into all of your content, whether it's a blog post, video, social media post, or email newsletter. One way to do this is to create a set of brand storytelling guidelines that outline the key elements of your narrative, such as the tone, voice, and key messaging.

You can create a set of characters or personas that represent different segments of your target audience and use them to create relatable stories. These stories should focus on the problems that your products or services solve for your customers.

Finally, you could also create a content calendar that aligns with the narrative and have a plan for the content that goes into different platforms. This will help ensure that your content is consistent and on-brand.

Make your content easily shareable.

One way to increase visibility and reach new audiences is to make sure that your content is easily shareable on social media and other platforms. This can be achieved by including social sharing buttons on your website and blog, which makes it easy for visitors to share your content with their own networks.

You can optimize your social media posts for sharing by including engaging headlines and images, along with a clear call-to-action asking your followers to share the post.

You should also consider the type of content that is more likely to be shared, such as infographics, videos and interactive content. Additionally, you can leverage social media scheduling tools that will help you to schedule your content on different platforms in advance. This will help to ensure that your content is being shared at the best times to reach the most people.

Create shareable assets such as quotes, statistics or images that can be easily shared. Finally, it is important to track the performance of your content on different platforms and using analytics tools to identify which content is getting the most engagement and sharing, so you can optimize your strategy accordingly.

Track the performance of your content.

Use analytics and data to track the performance of your content and identify which stories are resonating with your audience.

One way to do this is to set up tracking and measurement tools, such as Google Analytics, to monitor website traffic and engagement metrics.

Yyou should monitor social media analytics to track engagement, reach, and sharing on different platforms.

To refine your content strategy, you should regularly review and analyze the data you collect, paying close attention to metrics such as click-through rates, time spent on the page, and engagement rates.

Once you have identified which content is resonating with your audience, you can create more of that type of content and optimize your storytelling approach accordingly.

For example, if you notice that videos are particularly popular, you can create more videos that align with your narrative and focus on the topics and issues that are most important to your audience.

You can also use surveys, polls or feedback forms to get more insights from your audience and adjust your strategy accordingly.

Finally, it is important to use the data you collect to identify trends, patterns and opportunities to improve the effectiveness of your storytelling over time.

Invest in high-quality visuals.

Investing in high-quality visuals is a great way to enhance your stories and make them more engaging for your audience.

One key step to this is to develop a clear visual identity for your brand, which should include guidelines for color palettes, typography, and imagery. This will ensure a consistent look and feel across all of your content.

You should invest in professional photography and videography services to create high-quality visuals that align with your brand's visual identity and storytelling.

You can also consider hiring a dedicated photographer or videographer to capture behind-the-scenes footage, product demos, and other types of content that can be used across multiple channels. You can also use stock photos and videos, but make sure they align with your brand's visual identity and storytelling.

To make your visuals more engaging, you can use animation, infographics, and interactive elements to enhance your stories and add more visual appeal.

Finally, it is important to optimize your visuals for different platforms, such as social media, web, and email, to ensure that they look great and perform well on all devices.

Leverage the power of social media.

Leveraging the power of social media is an effective way to promote your content and engage with your audience.

One way to do this is to use platforms like Instagram and Facebook to share behind-the-scenes looks, customer testimonials, and other storytelling content that aligns with your brand's narrative.

To start, you should create a social media content calendar that aligns with your overall content strategy, this will ensure that your content is consistent across all channels.

You should use Instagram and Facebook's built-in analytics tools to track engagement, reach, and sharing on your posts, and adjust your strategy accordingly.

Another way to connect with your audience is by creating Instagram stories, IGTV or Facebook Live videos that give a behind-the-scenes look at your company, products, and services.

Leverage user-generated content by reposting customer testimonials, reviews, and other content that highlights the value of your products and services.

You could also use social media advertising to reach a wider audience and increase visibility for your content.

Finally, don't forget to engage with your audience by responding to comments, messages and direct messages, this will help you to build a deeper connection with your followers.

Encourage your audience to share their own stories.

Encouraging your audience to share their own stories of how your products and services have made a positive impact in their lives is a great way to create a sense of community and build trust with your audience. One way to do this is to create a dedicated space on your website, such as a customer testimonials page or social media hashtag, where customers can share their stories.

You can reach out to your customers and ask for their feedback and testimonials. You can also create a contest or incentive program to encourage customers to share their stories and reward those who participate.

Once you have collected user-generated content, you can use it in a variety of ways, such as creating social media posts, blog articles, videos, or infographics that highlight the positive impact your products and services have had on your customers' lives.

This type of content can be powerful in building trust with your audience, as it provides genuine, relatable examples of the value your products and services can provide.

You could use this content to create a sense of community among your customers by sharing their stories and highlighting their achievements.

Finally, make sure to always ask for permission before sharing any user-generated content and give proper credit to the original creator.

Communicate your brand's mission, values, and corporate social responsibility efforts.

Using storytelling to communicate your brand's mission, values, and corporate social responsibility (CSR) efforts is a powerful way to create a sense of purpose and meaning that resonates with your audience and drives business results.

To start, you should identify the key elements of your brand's mission and values, such as sustainability, community engagement, or ethical sourcing, and develop a narrative that aligns with these elements.

You should develop a set of guidelines for storytelling that align with your brand's mission and values, such as the tone, voice, and key messaging.

One way to effectively communicate your CSR efforts is to create a dedicated section on your website that highlights the initiatives you're undertaking and the impact they're having.

Create social media posts, blog articles, videos, or infographics that give a behind-the-scenes look at the initiatives and the people who are making them happen.

Also, you could use customer testimonials and case studies to show how your CSR efforts are making a positive impact on the lives of your customers and the communities in which you operate.

Make sure to align your CSR efforts with your overall business strategy and communicate them to your employees, suppliers, and other stakeholders. This will help to create a sense of shared purpose and ensure that everyone is working towards the same goals.

Finally, it is important to track the performance of your CSR storytelling and measure its impact on your business, using metrics such as website traffic, engagement, and customer feedback. This will help you to identify what's working and what isn't, and adjust your strategy accordingly.

connecting the dots

· · · · · · · ● · · · · · · · · · · ·

In this chapter, we dove into the world of content marketing and how incorporating storytelling can take your content to the next level.

By creating valuable and informative content that aligns with your brand's values and mission, you can attract and retain a clearly defined audience, ultimately driving profitable customer action. But simply providing useful information isn't enough.

In order to truly engage and connect with your audience, you need to tell a compelling story that resonates with them on an emotional level.

In the next chapter, we'll explore how storytelling can be used to create an emotional connection with customers and build trust and credibility.

chapter 8

Connecting With Customers On An Emotional Level Through Storytelling

• • • • • • • • ● • • • • • • • • • •

Once upon a time, in a land of magic and wonder, there was a brand of enchanted candles. The candles were crafted by a team of skilled sorceresses who took great care in selecting the finest ingredients and creating a variety of enchantments. The candles were popular with customers, but the brand struggled to create a deeper connection with them.

One day, a wise old sorceress named Estelle visited the brand and noticed their struggles. She explained to the sorceresses that in order to create a deeper connection with customers, they needed to connect with them on an emotional level through storytelling.

The sorceresses were intrigued by Estelle's advice and decided to give it a try. They created a storytelling strategy that focused on the emotions and feelings that their candles evoked. They shared stories of how their candles helped people to relax, to feel cozy and to create a sense of calm. They also shared stories of how the candles helped people to create a warm and inviting atmosphere in their homes.

As they began to share their stories, the sorceresses noticed a change in their customers. People were no longer just buying candles, they were buying a feeling, an emotion, and an experience. They began to create a deeper connection with their customers, as people felt like they were buying something that would make a positive impact in their lives.

Word of the brand's enchanted candles and their emotional stories began to spread throughout the land, and soon the brand became known for its ability to create a warm and inviting atmosphere.

The brand's sales increased, and it was able to expand its business and create jobs in the community.

Now that we've talked about the power of storytelling in content marketing, it's time to focus on how to really pull at your audience's heartstrings and create an emotional connection through storytelling.

By using authentic and relatable stories, you can create a deeper connection with your audience and make your brand stand out in a crowded market.

In Chapter 8, we're going to dive into the art of connecting with customers on an emotional level through storytelling and explore some examples of brands that are doing it right.

Whether you're just starting out with your brand or looking to take your marketing efforts to the next level, this chapter will provide valuable insights and tips for using storytelling to create an emotional connection with your customers.

Storytelling has the ability to connect with customers on an emotional level in a way that traditional marketing tactics cannot. By using stories to communicate your brand's values, mission, and message in an authentic and engaging way, you can create a deeper connection with your customers and build loyalty and trust.

In this chapter, we'll explore the powerful role that storytelling can play in building emotional connections with customers and how you can use it to create a strong and memorable brand.

It's important to stay up-to-date on the latest marketing trends and strategies, and storytelling through social media is definitely one you don't want to miss out on.

> *The stats speak for themselves - according to a study by Social Science Research Network, people who experience a brand's story through social media are 2.4 times more likely to remember the story and 1.5 times more likely to share it with others.*[19]
>
> *And let's not forget about content marketing - a survey by the Content Marketing Institute found that an impressive 89% of B2B marketers and 86% of B2C marketers use it as part of their overall marketing strategy.*[20]

By incorporating storytelling into your social media and content marketing efforts, you can create a deeper connection with your audience, increase brand awareness, and drive profitable customer action.

Don't let your business miss out on these powerful marketing opportunities!

Toyota

Tales Of Transformation And Fuel-Efficient Fun

Toyota is a company that has consistently used storytelling to create powerful and memorable experiences for its customers.

One key way that Toyota has done this is by showcasing the personal and meaningful experiences offered by its products.

For example, the "Start Your Impossible" campaign was launched by Toyota in 2018 as part of the company's global brand vision, which aims to inspire and support people in achieving their dreams.

The campaign focused on the idea that mobility can help people overcome barriers and achieve their goals, and it featured a series of inspiring stories about people who have used Toyota products to achieve their dreams, such as wheelchair athletes and entrepreneurs who used Toyota vehicles to pursue their passions.

The campaign was implemented through a variety of channels, including television commercials, social media, and live events.

Overall, the "Start Your Impossible" campaign was highly successful in creating an emotional connection with its audience and reinforcing Toyota's brand message of empowering people to achieve their goals.

Another example of Toyota's use of storytelling is the "Saved by Zero" campaign, which was used to promote the emotional benefits of driving a fuel-efficient vehicle.

Through this campaign, Toyota shared stories about the personal and environmental benefits of driving a fuel-efficient vehicle, such as saving money on fuel costs, reducing emissions, and making a positive impact on the environment.

By sharing stories about the personal and environmental benefits of driving a fuel-efficient vehicle, Toyota was able to create an emotional connection with its audience and showcase the values that are central to its brand identity.

Overall, Toyota's use of storytelling has been instrumental in helping the company create emotional connections with its customers and inspire loyalty.

Dove
Heartwarming Stories Of Empowerment And Self-Love

☐ wrinkled?
☐ wonderful?

Will society ever accept 'old' can be beautiful? Join the beauty de|

campaignforrealbeauty.co.uk 🕊 | D

Dove is a company that has consistently used storytelling to create emotional connections with its customers and inspire brand loyalty.

One key way that Dove has done this is by showcasing the personal and meaningful experiences offered by its products.

The "Real Beauty" campaign is a prime example of this, as it challenges traditional beauty standards and celebrates the unique qualities of real women.

It featured a series of advertisements that featured women of different ages, sizes, and skin tones, and used slogans like "Real Women Have Curves" and "Beauty Comes in All Shapes and Sizes."

The campaign was highly successful and has been credited with helping to shift societal perceptions of beauty and promote body positivity.

In addition to the advertisements, Dove also launched a number of initiatives in conjunction with the campaign, including the Dove Self-Esteem Fund and the Dove Real Beauty Pledge, which sought to promote self-esteem and encourage people to embrace their natural beauty.

Another example of Dove's use of storytelling is the "Love Your Curls" campaign, which was a multi-faceted campaign that included elements such as educational content on caring for natural curls, a social media challenge encouraging women to share their own natural curl journeys, and the launch of a new line of products specifically formulated for curly hair.

The campaign also featured real women sharing their own personal stories about embracing their natural curls and the confidence and self-love that came along with it.

Through this campaign, Dove aimed to promote body positivity and inclusivity, and to encourage women to celebrate their natural beauty.

By sharing stories about the personal and emotional benefits of loving and embracing one's natural curls, Dove was able to create an emotional connection with its audience and promote a positive and empowering message.

action guide

· · · · · · ● ● ● ● ● ● ● · · · · · · · ·

Having gained insight into the significance of connecting with your customers, let's examine actionable tactics for connecting with them on an emotional level:

Conduct market research.

It is essential to understand the emotions and feelings that your brand evokes in your customers. This understanding can inform the messaging and campaigns that you create, as well as how you interact with customers and how you approach customer service.

To gather this information, it is crucial to conduct market research and customer surveys. These can take many forms, such as online surveys, focus groups, or in-person interviews.

The key is to ask questions that are specifically designed to gather information about how your brand is perceived and what emotions it evokes.

Analyze the data you collect from these surveys and research to identify patterns and trends. Based on this information, you can then develop strategies to reinforce positive emotions and associations with your brand, or address any negative perceptions.

Tap into the emotions of your audience.

Creating stories that tap into the emotions of your audience is an effective way to build a strong connection with them and showcase the value of your brand or products.

One way to do this is by using storytelling to highlight how your brand or products have positively impacted the lives of your customers. This could include sharing customer testimonials, success stories, and case studies that demonstrate the tangible benefits that customers have experienced as a result of using your products or services.

To develop these stories, you can gather customer feedback and reviews, conduct interviews with satisfied customers, and look for patterns in the feedback you receive.

Another way to create stories is to use storytelling to showcase the values, mission, and vision of your brand. This way you can connect with your audience on a deeper level and help them understand the purpose behind your brand.

It is important to use a variety of different mediums to share these stories, such as video, social media, blog posts, or email marketing campaigns. This will help to ensure that your stories reach a wide audience and resonate with different segments of your target market.

Communicate the values and mission of your brand.

Using storytelling to communicate the values and mission of your brand can help to build a deeper connection with your audience and create a sense of purpose and meaning that resonates with them.

One way to do this is by sharing the story of how your brand came to be and the purpose behind it. This could include sharing the history of your company, the challenges you've faced, and the achievements you're proud of.

You can also share personal stories of the founders or key people involved in the company that can help to humanize the brand and give a sense of personal touch.

Use different mediums to share the story, such as social media, video, blog posts, or email campaigns.

Another way to use storytelling to communicate your brand values is by sharing stories that align with your brand's mission or purpose.

For example, if your brand's mission is to promote sustainable living, you could share stories of customers who have made environmentally-friendly choices and the impact it had on their lives. This way, you can connect your brand mission to the customer's real life and show them the real impact of their choices.

Additionally, you can also use storytelling to create a sense of community around your brand.

Share stories of customers who have formed connections or communities around your brand. This can help create a sense of belonging and make your audience feel like they are part of something bigger than themselves.

Use storytelling in all aspects of your marketing.

Incorporating storytelling into all aspects of your marketing can help to create a consistent and compelling narrative for your brand that resonates with your audience.

One way to do this is by including storytelling elements on your website. This could include using storytelling on your homepage, creating dedicated pages for customer testimonials or success stories, or using storytelling in product descriptions.

You can use storytelling in your social media marketing by sharing customer stories, behind-the-scenes content, and real-life examples of how your products or services are being used.

Another way to use storytelling in your marketing is through email marketing. You can include customer success stories, testimonials or case studies in your email campaigns, or use storytelling in the subject line or body of the email to grab the attention of your audience.

You can also use storytelling in other marketing materials such as brochures, flyers, and presentations.

For example, you can use storytelling to present a problem and the solution that your brand provides.

Use storytelling to present the benefits of your product or service in a way that connects with your audience's emotions.

Showcase your brand's commitment to causes.

Using storytelling to showcase your brand's commitment to social and environmental causes can help to build trust and credibility with your audience, as well as differentiate your brand from competitors.

One way to do this is by creating dedicated content that communicates your corporate social responsibility and sustainability efforts. This could include creating blog posts, videos, or social media campaigns that share stories of the specific actions your company is taking to support social and environmental causes.

It could also include sharing the impact of these actions, such as the number of lives impacted or the amount of carbon emissions reduced.

Another way to use storytelling to communicate your corporate social responsibility and sustainability efforts is by including them in your brand messaging and marketing materials.

For example, you can include information about your sustainability efforts in your product packaging, website, or email marketing campaigns.

You can use storytelling to communicate your brand's values, mission, or vision and how they align with social and environmental causes. This way, you can connect your brand's purpose with the causes you support and create a deeper sense of meaning and purpose for your audience.

Create a consistent brand voice and message.

Using storytelling to create a consistent brand voice and message can help to establish a strong and recognizable identity for your brand, and create a sense of familiarity and trust with your audience.

One way to do this is by developing a set of guidelines for your brand's storytelling approach, including the tone, style, and messaging. This will help ensure that all of your storytelling efforts are aligned and consistent with your overall brand identity.

Use storytelling to create a consistent voice across all of your marketing channels, such as website, social media, email marketing, and other marketing materials.

Another way to use storytelling to create a consistent brand voice and message is by using the same protagonist or characters in your stories.

For example, you can use the same customer or employee in multiple stories to create a sense of familiarity and consistency.

You can also use storytelling to communicate your brand values and mission, and how they align with your audience's values and beliefs. This way, you can create a deeper sense of connection and trust with your audience.

Highlight the emotional impact of your products and services.

Using storytelling to create emotional connections with your customers can help to build a deeper and more meaningful relationship with them, making them feel like they are an integral part of your brand's story.

One way to do this is by sharing customer stories that highlight the emotional impact of your products or services. This could include sharing customer testimonials, success stories, or case studies that demonstrate how your products or services have positively impacted customers' lives.

Use storytelling to create a sense of community around your brand by sharing stories of customers who have formed connections or communities around your brand, which can help create a sense of belonging and make your audience feel like they are part of something bigger than themselves.

Another way to use storytelling to create emotional connections with your customers is by creating content that evokes specific emotions.

For example, you can use storytelling to create a sense of nostalgia, excitement, or inspiration.

Communicate the values, mission, and vision of your brand and how they align with your customers' values and beliefs. This way, you can create a deeper sense of connection and understanding with your audience.

Improve customer engagement.

Using storytelling to improve customer engagement can help to create a deeper sense of connection and loyalty with your customers, and make them feel like they are a part of your brand's journey.

One way to do this is by encouraging customers to share their own stories and experiences with your brand. This could include creating a dedicated space on your website or social media channels where customers can share their stories, running a customer-generated content campaign, or hosting an event where customers can share their experiences in person.

By giving customers a platform to share their stories, you can create a sense of community and make your customers feel like they are an integral part of your brand.

Another way to use storytelling to improve customer engagement is by creating a sense of personalization.

Communicate with your customers in a way that is relatable and personalized to them.

For example, you can use storytelling to create personalized emails or messages that include a customer's name, preferences, or purchase history.

You can also use storytelling to create personalized offers or promotions that are tailored to a customer's specific interests or needs.

Measure the success of your storytelling efforts.

Measuring the success of your storytelling efforts is an essential step to ensure that your stories are resonating with your target audience and achieving your desired objectives.

One way to do this is by using analytics and metrics to track engagement and interaction with your stories. This could include tracking the number of views, shares, likes, and comments on your stories, as well as the click-through rates and conversion rates on your marketing campaigns.

You can also use tools such as Google Analytics or social media analytics to track the effectiveness of your storytelling efforts across different platforms and channels.

Another way to measure the success of your storytelling efforts is by conducting surveys or focus groups to gather customer feedback. This could include asking customers about their perceptions of your brand, or the impact of your stories on their purchasing decisions. You can also use customer feedback to identify patterns or themes in the feedback you receive and make adjustments as needed.

connecting the dots

By understanding the emotional needs and desires of your audience and crafting authentic and engaging stories that tap into those emotions, you can create powerful and memorable experiences that inspire loyalty and drive business results.

As we've learned, storytelling is a powerful tool for businesses looking to connect with their customers and create a memorable brand experience.

But beyond creating emotional connections and building brand loyalty, storytelling can also be used to establish trust and credibility with your audience.

In Chapter 9, we will explore the ways in which storytelling can help businesses build trust and credibility with their customers, and how you can use storytelling to communicate your brand's values and mission in an authentic and engaging way.

By leveraging the power of storytelling, businesses can not only connect with their customers on an emotional level, but also establish trust and credibility that will help them stand out in a crowded market.

chapter 9

Building Trust And Credibility
With Storytelling

· · · · · · · · ●· · · · · · · · · · ·

Once upon a time, in a kingdom of myths and legends, there was a brand of magical potions. The potions were crafted by a team of skilled alchemists who took great care in selecting the finest ingredients and creating a variety of powerful formulas. The potions were a hit with customers, but the brand struggled to build trust and credibility with them.

One day, a wise old sorcerer named Dumbledore visited the brand and noticed their struggles. He explained to the alchemists that in order to build trust and credibility with customers, they needed to use storytelling to communicate the care and expertise that went into creating each potion.

The alchemists were intrigued by Dumbledore's advice and decided to give it a try. They created a storytelling strategy that focused on the care and expertise that went into creating each potion. They shared stories of the rigorous testing and quality control processes they used, the rare and powerful ingredients they sourced, and the positive impact their potions had on people's lives.

As they began to share their stories, the alchemists noticed a change in their customers. People began to see the brand as responsible, trustworthy, and expert in their field. They began to trust the brand and its potions, and they were willing to pay more for them because they felt like they were getting something special and of high quality.

Word of the brand's magical potions and their stories began to spread throughout the kingdom, and soon the brand became known for its responsible and trustworthy potions. The brand's sales increased and it was able to expand its business and create jobs in the community.

We all know that storytelling has long been a powerful tool for connecting with customers and creating a memorable brand experience.

But in today's digital age, where there's an endless stream of marketing messages coming at us from every direction, it's more important than ever to stand out and differentiate your brand. And that's where storytelling comes in.

By using storytelling to communicate your brand's values, mission, and message in an engaging and authentic way, you can create a strong brand identity that resonates with your target audience and helps you stand out in a crowded market.

But it doesn't stop there - storytelling can also help you establish trust and credibility with your customers.

We'll dive into the ways in which businesses can use storytelling to build trust and credibility with their audience, and how you can leverage the power of storytelling to communicate your brand's values and mission in an authentic and engaging way.

By using authentic and compelling stories, businesses can establish trust and credibility with their customers, ultimately driving sales and building loyalty.

In this chapter, we'll explore the various ways in which businesses can use storytelling to build trust and credibility with their customers.

It's no secret that emotional connections are key to building strong relationships with customers. And according to research, it's clear that storytelling is a powerful tool for making that emotional connection.

> *In fact, a study by the Nielsen Group found that 63% of consumers are more likely to purchase from a brand that they feel emotionally connected to.[21]*
>
> *Plus, a separate study by content marketing software provider Contently discovered that businesses that use storytelling in their marketing efforts can increase customer loyalty by a whopping 20%.[22]*

But it's not just about building loyalty - storytelling can also help businesses differentiate themselves from their competitors and establish a unique brand identity.

By using storytelling to connect with their customers on an emotional level and showcase their values and mission, businesses can not only build a loyal customer base, but also establish themselves as a trusted and credible brand.

So don't underestimate the power of storytelling - it could be the key to building strong, long-lasting relationships with your customers.

Southwest

Embracing Inclusion And Democratizing The Skies

At the heart of Southwest's brand story is the idea of democratizing air travel and making it accessible to all.

This message is consistently communicated through marketing campaigns and customer interactions, using storytelling to connect with their audience on an emotional level.

One example of Southwest's use of storytelling is the company's advertising campaign that featured real employees telling their own stories about the company's commitment to inclusivity and diversity.

By featuring real employees sharing their own personal stories about their experiences at the company, Southwest was able to create an authentic and relatable connection with its audience.

This campaign likely helped to build trust and credibility with customers and further solidify Southwest's brand identity as a company that values inclusivity. It may have also resonated with customers who prioritize diversity and inclusion in their purchasing decisions.

Additionally, this campaign could have had a powerful impact on Southwest employees themselves, as it provided them with an opportunity to share their own stories and experiences.

This could have helped to foster a sense of community and belonging within the company, and may have even inspired other employees to share their own stories as well.

By highlighting the diverse backgrounds and experiences of its employees, Southwest was able to showcase the rich tapestry of perspectives and experiences that make up its workforce.

This could have not only attracted potential customers, but also attracted top talent to the company.

Overall, the "real employees" campaign was a creative and effective way for Southwest to communicate its values and connect with its audience on an emotional level.

In addition to using storytelling in its marketing efforts, Southwest has also consistently incorporated it into its customer interactions.

From friendly and helpful customer service to onboard experiences that reflect the company's fun and laid-back brand personality, Southwest has used storytelling to create a memorable and enjoyable customer experience.

Patagonia

Where Sustainability Meets Style

· · · · · · ●●●●●● ● ●●●●●● · · · · ·

Patagonia is a company that has consistently used storytelling to engage with its customers and communicate its brand identity.

At the heart of their brand narrative is a strong commitment to sustainability and environmental conservation.

In addition to using sustainable materials in their products, Patagonia also uses their platform to raise awareness about environmental issues and encourage their customers to take action.

One key way that Patagonia has used storytelling to connect with its audience is by transparently sharing the stories of their products and supply chain with their customers.

On their website, they have a "Footprint Chronicles" section, an online resource that aims to increase transparency and accountability in the company's supply chain.

It includes detailed information about the materials used in Patagonia's products, the environmental impact of those materials, and the company's efforts to reduce their environmental footprint.

One key aspect of the "Footprint Chronicles" section is the Life Cycle Assessment (LCA) tool, which allows customers to see the environmental impact of a specific product throughout its entire lifecycle, from raw material extraction to disposal.

This information includes data on energy use, water usage, greenhouse gas emissions, and other environmental indicators.

By sharing this level of detail about their supply chain and products, Patagonia is able to showcase their commitment to sustainability and provide customers with the information they need to make informed purchasing decisions.

This level of transparency helps to build trust with their customers and showcase their commitment to sustainability.

In addition to sharing the stories of their products and supply chain, Patagonia also uses storytelling to engage with their customers on an emotional level.

Whether through showcasing the personal and meaningful experiences offered by their products or highlighting the impact of their sustainability efforts, Patagonia consistently uses storytelling to create powerful and memorable experiences for their audience.

action guide

·········●··········

Now that the importance of building trust and credibility is clear, let's proceed to actionable methods for constructing credible stories:

Craft authentic and engaging stories.

To craft authentic and engaging stories about your products and services, it is important to first identify the unique features and benefits that set them apart from your competitors.

Once you have a clear understanding of what makes your products and services special, you can begin to craft stories that highlight these features and benefits in a relatable and credible way.

One effective way to do this is to use real-life examples and customer testimonials.

For example, you could create a case study that shares the story of how one of your customers used your product or service to solve a specific problem, or you could create a customer testimonial video that shows a happy customer sharing their positive experience with your brand.

You can also use social media platforms, such as Instagram or YouTube, to post customer stories, or you can collaborate with influencers to showcase how your product or service can be used in various settings.

Another approach is to start storytelling campaigns, which can be in the form of videos, infographics, or written content that tells a story of how your product or service can change a customer's life.

It is also important to use storytelling throughout the customer journey, from the first time they hear about your brand to the moment they become a loyal customer. This can be done through website copy, email marketing, and even in-store displays.

Communicate the care and expertise that goes into creating your products and services.

Using storytelling to communicate the care and expertise that goes into creating your products and services can be a powerful way to build trust and credibility with your customers.

One specific action step you can take is to share stories about your rigorous testing and quality control processes.

For example, you could create a video that takes viewers behind the scenes of your manufacturing facility, highlighting the various tests and inspections your products go through before they are deemed ready for sale.

Another approach is to create an infographic that illustrates the different stages of quality control your products go through, with accompanying descriptions of how each step ensures that your products meet the highest standards of quality.

Communicate the care and expertise that goes into your products and services is by highlighting the rare and powerful ingredients you use. Share the story of where these ingredients come from, the care taken in sourcing them, and their unique properties that make your products effective.

Finally, you can use storytelling to communicate the positive impact your products have on people's lives.

Share real-life stories of customers who have seen improvement in their skin, hair, or overall health thanks to your product, or feature case studies or testimonials from customers who have experienced the benefits of your product or service first-hand.

Create a sense of purpose and meaning.

Using storytelling to tap into the emotions of your audience can be a powerful way to create a sense of purpose and meaning for your brand.

One specific action step you can take is to share stories that evoke feelings of trust and reliability.

For example, you could create a video that shares the story of how your company has been in business for several decades, highlighting the long-standing relationships you've built with customers and suppliers over the years.

Another approach is to create a written case study that shares the story of a customer who has been using your products or services for years and has seen consistent results.

Use storytelling to tap into the emotions of your audience is by sharing stories that evoke feelings of positivity.

For example, you could create a video that highlights the charitable work your company does, or a series of social media posts that feature your customers sharing their positive experiences with your brand.

You can also use storytelling to showcase your brand's values, and the impact it has on the society. Share stories of how your brand is contributing to the community, or making a positive impact on the environment.

Communicate your corporate social responsibility and sustainability efforts.

Using storytelling to communicate your corporate social responsibility and sustainability efforts can be a powerful way to build trust and credibility with your customers and stakeholders.

One specific action step you can take is to share stories about your commitment to social and environmental causes.

For example, you could create a video that highlights your company's support for a specific social cause, such as education or poverty reduction, or you could create a written case study that shares the story of how your company has implemented sustainable practices in your operations.

Another way to use storytelling to communicate your corporate social responsibility and sustainability efforts is by sharing stories about how your products and services contribute to making the world a better place.

For example, you could create a series of social media posts that feature customers using your products in an environmentally friendly way, or you could create a blog post that shares the story of how your company has been working to reduce its carbon footprint.

You can also use storytelling to communicate your company's impact on the society. Share stories of how your brand is impacting the community positively, or how you are actively working towards sustainable development goals.

Leverage the power of social media.

Leveraging the power of social media to tell your brand's story and engage with your audience is a powerful way to create meaningful connections and drive business results.

One specific action step you can take is to create compelling and engaging content that resonates with your audience.

For example, you could create a series of social media posts that feature behind-the-scenes content that gives your followers a glimpse into the day-to-day operations of your company, or you could create a social media campaign that features customer testimonials or success stories.

Another way to use social media to tell your brand's story and engage with your audience is by creating engaging visual content, such as videos, infographics, or images that showcase your products or services in action.

Use social media platforms to host live sessions, webinars, or Q&A sessions that allow your audience to interact with you in real-time.

You can also use social media to share stories of your company's culture, values, and mission, as well as any corporate social responsibility or sustainability efforts.

Another important step is to listen to your audience, and engage with them by responding to comments and messages, and sharing user-generated content. This will help you build a relationship with your audience and understand what resonates with them.

Create compelling and engaging content.

Using storytelling in your content marketing strategy is a powerful way to create compelling and engaging content that resonates with your audience.

One specific action step you can take is to use storytelling to create content that adds value to your audience.

For example, you could create a blog post that shares the story of how one of your customers used your product or service to solve a specific problem, or you could create a video that shares the story of how your company has been working to improve its sustainability practices. This type of content not only educates your audience about your products and services, but it also demonstrates your company's expertise and values.

Another way to use storytelling in your content marketing strategy is by creating content that entertains your audience.

For example, you could create a series of social media posts that feature humorous or lighthearted stories about your company or your employees, or you could create a video that shares the story of how your company came up with a new product idea. This type of content helps to humanize your brand and make it more relatable to your audience.

You can also use storytelling to create a sense of community among your audience. Share stories of how your customers have been impacted positively by your products and services. This will help them feel connected to your brand, and they will be more likely to be loyal customers.

Maintain consistency in your storytelling.

Maintaining consistency in your storytelling is crucial to building a sense of familiarity and trust with your audience.

One specific action step you can take is to use a consistent brand voice and message across all of your communications. This means that all of the stories you tell, whether they are in written or video form, should have a similar tone, language, and style. This will help to establish a recognizable and memorable brand voice that your audience can identify with.

Another specific action step to maintain consistency in storytelling is to use a consistent message across all of your communications.

This means that all of your stories should be aligned with your overall brand message and should communicate the same core values and benefits of your products or services. This will help to ensure that your audience is receiving a consistent message and can easily understand what your brand stands for.

You can also maintain consistency in storytelling by using a similar format for all your stories.

For example, if you are using a story format that is a customer testimonial, make sure all your customer testimonials follow a similar structure and format. This will help to create a sense of familiarity and consistency for your audience.

Make sure that your stories align with your overall marketing strategy and goals. This will help to ensure that all your stories are working towards the same goals and objectives.

Encourage customers to share their own stories.

Encouraging customers to share their own stories about how your products and services have made a positive impact in their lives can be a powerful way to build trust and credibility with your audience.

One specific action step you can take is to create a system for collecting customer stories. This can be done by setting up a dedicated email address or online form where customers can submit their stories, or by creating a social media hashtag that customers can use to share their stories.

Another specific action step is to actively promote the submission of customer stories. This can be done by including a call-to-action on your website or in your email signature, encouraging customers to share their stories and highlighting the benefits of doing so.

Once you have collected customer stories, make sure to share them on your website, social media channels, and other marketing materials. This can be done through a dedicated page on your website, a blog post, a video, or by sharing customer stories as social media posts.

Another way to use customer stories is to create a case study, a written or video story that goes more in-depth about a customer's experience with your products or services, and how it solved their problem. This will give your audience a more detailed look at how your products or services have made a positive impact on the lives of others.

You can also use customer stories to create a sense of community among your audience. Share stories of how your customers have been impacted positively by your products and services. This will help them feel connected to your brand, and they will be more likely to be loyal customers.

connecting the dots

· · · · · · · · ● · · · · · · · · · · ·

In this chapter, we explored how storytelling can be used to build trust and credibility with customers. In Chapter 10, we'll take a closer look at how storytelling can be used to communicate a company's commitment to corporate social responsibility (CSR) and sustainability.

As consumers become more aware of the impact their purchases have on the environment and society, it's important for businesses to be transparent about their efforts in these areas.

By using storytelling to communicate their CSR and sustainability efforts, businesses can not only demonstrate their commitment to these issues, but also create a deeper connection with their customers and establish trust.

In the next chapter, we'll dive into the role of storytelling in CSR and sustainability and provide examples of companies that are doing it well.

chapter 10

The Role of Storytelling in Corporate Social Responsibility and Sustainability

· · · · · · ●●●● ● ●●●●● · · · · · ·

Once upon a time, in a land of magic and wonder, there was a brand of enchanted clothing. The clothing was crafted by a team of skilled tailors who took great care in selecting the finest materials and creating a variety of unique designs. The brand was successful, but the tailors realized that they needed to do more to ensure that their business was sustainable and had a positive impact on the community.

One day, a wise old sorcerer named Rowan visited the brand and noticed their desire to make a positive impact. He explained to the tailors that in order to communicate their commitment to sustainability and corporate social responsibility, they needed to use storytelling to share their values and actions with their customers.

The tailors were inspired by Rowan's advice and decided to develop a storytelling strategy that focused on their commitment to sustainability and corporate social responsibility. They shared stories of their efforts to use eco-friendly materials, their partnership with local artisans, and the positive impact their clothing had on the community.

As they began to share their stories, the tailors noticed a change in their customers. People began to see the brand as responsible and environmentally conscious. They began to trust the brand and its clothing, and they were willing to pay more for them because they felt like they were supporting a brand that had a positive impact on the community and the environment.

Word of the brand's enchanted clothing and their stories of sustainability and corporate social responsibility began to spread throughout the kingdom, and soon the brand became known for its commitment to making a positive impact. The brand's sales increased and it was able to expand its business and create jobs in the community while being sustainable.

Now that you've learned about the power of storytelling in building trust and credibility, let's dive into how it can be used to communicate a company's commitment to corporate social responsibility (CSR) and sustainability.

As consumers become more aware of the impact their purchases have on the environment and society, it's important for businesses to be transparent about their efforts in these areas. And what better way to do that than through storytelling?

By using authentic and engaging stories to showcase their CSR and sustainability efforts, businesses can not only demonstrate their commitment to these issues, but also create a deeper emotional connection with their customers.

But it's not just about showing off your good deeds – it's also about incorporating CSR and sustainability into the core of your brand.

By weaving these values into your brand's story, you can create a stronger and more authentic brand identity that resonates with customers who care about these issues.

In this chapter, we will explore the role of storytelling in corporate social responsibility and sustainability and how businesses can use it to create a positive impact and connect with their audience.

With the rise of the conscious consumer, it's no secret that people are becoming more and more interested in supporting businesses that are doing their part for the planet.

In fact, a study by Nielsen found that 66% of consumers are willing to pay more for products and services from companies that are socially and environmentally responsible.[23]

And when it comes to communicating those efforts to your audience, storytelling is key. Not only does it allow you to share your brand's values and mission in a relatable and authentic way, but research has also shown that storytelling can increase customer loyalty and trust.

So, if you're looking to connect with your audience and showcase your commitment to CSR and sustainability, consider incorporating storytelling into your marketing strategy.

The Body Shop

Sustainability Is In The Bag

The Body Shop is a company that has consistently used storytelling to engage with its customers and communicate its brand values and mission.

Founded in 1976 by Anita Roddick, The Body Shop has always been a leader in ethical and sustainable business practices.

From using natural and ethically-sourced ingredients in their products, to campaigning against animal testing in the cosmetics industry, The Body Shop has always used storytelling to share their commitment to sustainability and social responsibility.

One of the most memorable campaigns was the "Save the Whales" campaign, which used storytelling to raise awareness about the threat of whaling and the importance of protecting marine life.

Through this campaign, The Body Shop was able to not only raise funds for conservation efforts, but also build a strong emotional connection with their customers by telling a compelling and impactful story.

The campaign helped to strengthen The Body Shop's brand identity as a socially and environmentally responsible company, and may have also resonated with customers who prioritize sustainability and conservation in their purchasing decisions.

In addition to using storytelling in their marketing efforts, The Body Shop has also consistently incorporated their values and mission into their business practices.

By prioritizing sustainability and ethical sourcing, The Body Shop has been able to differentiate itself in the crowded cosmetics industry and build a loyal customer base.

Overall, The Body Shop's use of storytelling has played a key role in helping the company build a strong and cohesive brand identity that resonates with its target audience.

Seventh Generation

Eco-Friendly Products With A Story To Tell

Seventh Generation is a company that has consistently used storytelling as a way to communicate their values and practices to consumers.

Through their "Transparency List" and "Life Cycle Assessment," Seventh Generation has been able to provide detailed information about their products and the environmental impact of their production processes.

The "Transparency List" is a feature on their website that provides detailed information about the ingredients in their household and personal care products.

By sharing this information with their customers, Seventh Generation is able to demonstrate their commitment to transparency and honesty.

The "Life Cycle Assessment" is another feature on Seventh Generation's website that provides information about the environmental impact of their products throughout their entire lifecycle, from raw material extraction to disposal.

This includes information about the energy and water usage, as well as the carbon emissions associated with each product.

By sharing this information with their customers, Seventh Generation is able to demonstrate their commitment to sustainability and help consumers make informed purchasing decisions.

By consistently sharing this information, they are able to build trust and credibility with their audience.

In addition to these transparency efforts, Seventh Generation also regularly shares stories about their partnerships with organizations and initiatives that align with their values, as well as their own internal sustainability efforts.

For example, the company frequently shares stories about their work with organizations that promote environmental conservation and social justice, as well as their own efforts to reduce their carbon footprint and use sustainable materials in their products.

This approach to storytelling has helped Seventh Generation build trust and credibility with their audience and differentiate themselves in the crowded market for eco-friendly household and personal care products.

action guide

· · · · · · ●●●● ● ●●●● · · · · · ·

Given your comprehension of the magnitude of this chapter, let's discuss some actionable approaches:

Identify causes that align with your brand.

Identify specific social and environmental causes that align with your brand's values and mission. This can help to increase brand awareness, as well as demonstrate to your customers that your company is committed to making a positive impact on the world.

To identify specific causes, you can start by conducting a thorough analysis of your brand's mission, values, and target audience. This will help you to identify the issues that are most important to your customers and to your company.

Once you have identified a cause, you can then develop a plan to support it. This could include partnering with organizations that are already working to address the issue, or creating your own initiatives to raise awareness and funds.

It is important to communicate your efforts to your customers. This can be done through social media, email campaigns, and other marketing channels.

For example, if your brand values sustainability, you might consider partnering with a local organization that promotes sustainable farming practices or investing in renewable energy sources for your own operations.

If your brand is focused on community building, you can look for ways to support local community organizations or initiatives that help to strengthen the bonds within your community.

In both cases, it is important to communicate your efforts to your audience and to make it clear that your brand is taking a stand on these issues.

You can also look for ways to integrate these causes into your products or services, such as by using eco-friendly materials or by designing products that are made to last longer.

Showcase your commitment to these causes.

Develop stories that showcase your commitment to social and environmental causes and the actions your brand is taking to make a positive impact. These stories can take many forms, including written content, video, or images, and should be used to communicate your brand's values and mission to your target audience.

To develop these stories, you can start by identifying specific examples of the actions your brand is taking to support the causes you have chosen. This could include information about partnerships you have formed with organizations, initiatives you have launched, or specific products or services you have developed that align with your cause.

Once you have identified these examples, you can then use them to create compelling stories that highlight the positive impact your brand is making.

For example, if your brand is committed to reducing carbon emissions, you can create a story that highlights the steps you are taking to become more sustainable, such as investing in renewable energy sources or reducing your company's waste. This story can be accompanied by images or videos that show the specific actions your brand is taking and the positive impact they are having on the environment.

Additionally, you can also use customer testimonials to further highlight the positive impact of your actions.

Share these stories online.

Share the stories you've developed that showcase your commitment to social and environmental causes and the actions your brand is taking to make a positive impact across your website and social media channels to increase awareness and engagement with your audience.

By sharing these stories, you can use storytelling to create a sense of purpose and meaning that resonates with your audience, and inspire them to take action and support your brand.

To share these stories, you can start by creating a dedicated section on your website that highlights the causes you support and the actions your brand is taking to make a positive impact. This section should include written content, images, and videos that tell the story of your brand's commitment to these causes.

You can also create social media posts that share these stories, and use hashtags and other tools to increase visibility and engagement.

For example, if your brand is committed to supporting local communities, you can create a section on your website that highlights the specific initiatives you have launched to support local organizations and the positive impact they are having.

Additionally, you can create social media posts that share stories and images of these initiatives, and use hashtags such as #SupportLocal or #CommunitySupport to increase visibility and engagement.

Create a sense of trust and credibility with your audience.

Use storytelling to create a sense of trust and credibility with your audience by sharing the specific actions you are taking to support social and environmental causes, and also showcasing the positive impact these actions are having on the communities and causes you are supporting. This can help to build trust and credibility with your audience by demonstrating that your brand is truly committed to making a positive impact and is taking tangible steps to do so.

To use storytelling in this way, you can start by identifying specific examples of the actions your brand is taking to support the causes you have chosen. This could include information about partnerships you have formed with organizations, initiatives you have launched, or specific products or services you have developed that align with your cause.

Once you have identified these examples, you can then use them to create compelling stories that highlight the positive impact your brand is making.

For example, if your brand is committed to reducing carbon emissions, you can create a story that highlights the specific steps you are taking to become more sustainable, such as investing in renewable energy sources or reducing your company's waste.

Create a sense of purpose and meaning.

Use storytelling to create a sense of purpose and meaning that inspires loyalty and drives business results by highlighting the positive impact your brand is having in the world. This can help to build a strong emotional connection with your audience, which can lead to increased loyalty and ultimately drive business results.

To use storytelling in this way, you can start by identifying specific examples of the positive impact your brand is having on the world. This could include information about the causes you support, the initiatives you have launched, or the specific products or services you have developed that align with your cause.

Once you have identified these examples, you can then use them to create compelling stories that highlight the positive impact your brand is making.

For example, if your brand is committed to supporting local communities, you can create a story that highlights the specific initiatives you have launched to support local organizations, and how it has positively impacted the community.

Create a consistent narrative.

Create a consistent narrative throughout all of your storytelling efforts and be transparent and authentic in your messaging to build trust and credibility with your audience, and inspire them to take action and support your brand.

Consistency and authenticity in messaging will help to ensure that your audience understands your brand's values and mission and how it aligns with the causes you support.

To create a consistent narrative, you can start by developing a brand messaging guide that outlines the key messaging points you want to convey, and the tone and style of your storytelling efforts. This guide should include information on your brand's mission and values, the causes you support, and the specific actions your brand is taking to make a positive impact.

Once you have developed this guide, you can then use it to create consistent messaging across all of your storytelling efforts, whether they are on your website, social media channels, or other marketing materials.

To be transparent and authentic, it's important to be honest and open about the actions your brand is taking to support the causes you have chosen. This includes being transparent about any challenges or obstacles you may have faced, and how you have overcome them.

You can also use customer testimonials and statistics to further showcase the impact of your actions and how it has positively impacted the lives of your audience.

connecting the dots

· · · · · · · · ● · · · · · · · · · ·

The role of storytelling in corporate social responsibility and sustainability is crucial for businesses looking to create a positive impact and connect with consumers on a deeper level.

Whether through content marketing, social media, or traditional media, storytelling is a powerful tool for communicating a company's values and mission in a way that resonates with its audience.

As consumers become increasingly conscious of the impact of their purchasing decisions, the role of storytelling in corporate social responsibility and sustainability will only continue to grow in importance.

conclusion

The Future of Resilient Brands is Storytelling

· · · · · · ●●●●●●●●●●●● · · · ·

Are you up for the challenge?

With this guide, you now have the necessary case studies and tools to transform your brand into a resilient identity.

Over the last ten chapters, we've covered a lot of ground and explored the importance of crafting authentic and engaging narratives that connect with your audience on an emotional level. More importantly, we've outlined steps to help your brand stay relevant and thrive in the digital age.

I've constructed a recap of each chapter, along with the recommended action plan. Think of it as your very own cheat sheet:

chapter 1 cheat sheet

First things first, we learned in Chapter 1 that storytelling is a major key when it comes to creating a strong and cohesive brand identity. By crafting authentic and engaging stories that showcase your products and services, you can create a sense of purpose and meaning that inspires loyalty and drives business results.

To apply the lessons learned in this chapter, implement the following action plan:

- **Define your brand's story:**

  Start by identifying the key elements of your brand's story, such as its mission, values, and unique selling points. This will serve as the foundation for all of your storytelling efforts and help you to craft authentic and engaging stories that showcase your products and services.

- **Highlight the unique features and benefits:**

  Make sure to highlight the unique features and benefits of your products and services in your stories. This will help to differentiate your brand from your competitors and create a sense of excitement and desire among your audience.

- **Tap into emotions:**

  Use storytelling to tap into the emotions of your audience. By connecting with your audience on an emotional level, you can create a sense of purpose and meaning that inspires loyalty and drives business results. This can be achieved by highlighting the positive impact your products and services have on people's lives and using emotional language and imagery in your stories.

- **Use storytelling across all channels:**

  Utilize storytelling across all channels, including your website, social media, email marketing, and PR. This will help to create a consistent brand voice and message and ensure that your audience is exposed to your stories regardless of where they come into contact with your brand.

- **Encourage customer engagement:**

  Encourage customer engagement by inviting them to share their own stories about how your products and services have made a positive impact on their lives. This will help to create a sense of community and trust among your audience and will also provide valuable feedback that can be used to improve your products and services.

- **Use storytelling in product development:**

  Use storytelling in product development process by considering the story that each product tells. Think about the emotions that the product evokes, and how it can be used to improve people's lives. This will help to ensure that your products and services align with your brand's story and mission.

- **Measure the effectiveness of your storytelling:**

  Measure the effectiveness of your storytelling by tracking metrics such as website traffic, social media engagement, and customer satisfaction. Use this data to identify what is working well and what areas need improvement, and adjust your storytelling strategy accordingly.

- **Continuously update and refresh your stories:**

  Continuously update and refresh your stories to keep them relevant and interesting. Reflect on new developments and changes in your industry or market and adapt your stories accordingly.

· · · · · · ● · · · · · · · · · ·

chapter 2 cheat sheet

Chapter 2 was all about customer stories and how to use them to showcase the value of your products and services. By highlighting real-life examples of customers using your products and services, you can create a sense of trust and credibility with your audience.

To apply the lessons learned in this chapter, implement the following action plan:

- **Identify your most satisfied customers:**

  These are the customers who have experienced the most success with your products or services and are likely to be the most vocal about their positive experiences.

- **Ask customers to share their stories:**

  Ask if they would be willing to share their story. Make sure to explain how their story will be used and how it will benefit them (e.g. by being featured on your website or social media channels).

- **Showcase their experience with your products or services:**

  Make sure to highlight the specific challenges they faced and how your products or services helped them overcome those challenges.

- **Make the customer stories engaging and relatable:**

  Use storytelling techniques, such as setting the scene, creating a character, and using a clear narrative structure.

- **Share the stories across multiple channels:**

  Post on your website, social media, email marketing, and in-store.

- **Encourage customers to share their stories with others:**

  Include social sharing buttons or create a referral program.

- **Measure the results of your customer stories:**

  Track engagement, sales and website traffic. Use the data to improve and refine your storytelling efforts.

- **Continuously gather customer feedback:**

  Reflect the most recent and relevant experiences of your customers.

- **Align your customer stories align with your brand values:**

  Ensure that they are consistent with the rest of your marketing efforts.

· · · · · · ●●●●●●●●●●●●●●●●● · · ·

chapter 3 cheat sheet

In Chapter 3, we dove into your brand's origin story and why it's more than just a boring history lesson. By sharing your brand's journey and values, you can connect with customers on an emotional level and inspire loyalty.

To apply the lessons learned in this chapter, implement the following action plan:

- **Identify the key elements of your origin story:**

  This could include the founding of the company, any major milestones or turning points, and the values and mission that drive the brand.

- **Develop an engaging and authentic narrative:**

  Make sure to highlight the emotional connection that your brand has with its customers, and how it aims to make a positive impact in the world.

- **Share your origin story across multiple channels:**

  You can use your website, social media, video content, and other marketing materials to share the story with your audience.

- **Incorporate your origin story into your marketing efforts:**

  Use it to create a consistent message and image that reflects your brand's values and mission.

- **Create a special landing page dedicated to your origin story:**

  Help people can learn more about your brand, its mission and its values.

- **Build a deeper connection with your customers:**

  Share the stories of the people behind the brand, their personal journey and the values they believe in.

- **Create a sense of community around your brand:**

  Encourage customers to share their own stories and experiences with your brand, and use it to create a sense of belonging and connection among your customers.

· · · · · · · · ● · · · · · · · · · · ·

chapter 4 cheat sheet

Chapter 4 was all about product stories and how to use them to showcase the value of your products and services. By highlighting the unique features and benefits of your products, you can create a sense of excitement and desire among your audience.

To apply the lessons learned in this chapter, implement the following action plan:

- **Identify the unique features and benefits of your products:**

  Before you can effectively highlight the value of your products, you need to know what makes them unique. Take the time to identify the key features and benefits of your products that set them apart from your competitors.

- **Tell a story:**

  Instead of simply listing the features and benefits of your products, use storytelling to create a narrative around them. This will help your audience to envision themselves using your products and see how they can improve their lives.

- **Use visuals:**

  Use high-quality images and videos to showcase your products in action. This will help to create a sense of excitement and desire among your audience.

- **Create a sense of scarcity:**

  Use storytelling to create a sense of urgency around your products. Highlight the limited availability or the exclusivity of your products to create a sense of scarcity.

- **Use customer testimonials:**

  Incorporating customer testimonials into your product stories can be a powerful way to add credibility to your claims and create social proof.

- **Use emotional appeal:**

  Use storytelling to tap into the emotions of your audience by highlighting how your products can help improve their lives.

- **Use humor:**

  Humor can be a powerful tool to create a sense of excitement and desire among your audience. Use storytelling to add a humorous twist to your product stories.

- **Create a sense of mystery:**

  Use storytelling to create a sense of mystery around your products, this will make the audience more curious and eager to know more.

chapter 5 cheat sheet

We learned about the importance of consistency in storytelling in Chapter 5. By maintaining a consistent brand voice and message, you can create a sense of familiarity and trust with your audience.

To apply the lessons learned in this chapter, implement the following action plan:

- **Define your brand's unique voice and message:**

   This should include the tone, language, and overall messaging that you want to convey to your audience.

- **Create guidelines for your brand's voice and message:**

   These guidelines should be shared with all team members and should be used as a reference for all brand-related content, including social media posts, website copy, email campaigns, and more.

- **Train your team members on how to use the guidelines effectively:**

   This includes providing examples of how to use the guidelines in different types of content and reviewing their work to ensure consistency.

- **Regularly review your brand's voice and message:**

   This will help you identify any inconsistencies and make any necessary adjustments to ensure that your message is consistent across all channels.

- **Track the performance of your content:**

   Identify any areas where you need to improve consistency. This can include tracking engagement rates, website traffic, and conversion rates.

- **Use customer feedback to improve your brand's message:**

This can include conducting surveys, hosting focus groups, or conducting customer interviews to gain insight into how your customers perceive your brand.

- **Continually adapt your brand's voice and message as your business evolves:**

    As your business grows, your target audience and goals may change, and your messaging should reflect this.

· · · · · · · · · ● · · · · · · · · · ·

chapter 6 cheat sheet

In Chapter 6, we explored the power of social media and how to use it to tell your brand's story and engage with your audience. By leveraging the power of social media, you can create meaningful connections and drive business results.

To apply the lessons learned in this chapter, implement the following action plan:

- **Develop a social media strategy:**

    Focus on telling your brand's story through engaging and authentic content.

- **Highlight the unique features and benefits of your products and services:**

    Showcase the the unique features and benefits, and real-life examples of customers using them.

- **Share your brand's origin story:**

    Connect with customers on an emotional level and create a sense of purpose and meaning.

- **Listen to customer feedback:**

    Use it to improve your products and services.

- **Track engagement and reach:**

  Track the engagement and reach of your storytelling content and adjust your strategy accordingly.

- **Create a consistent brand voice and message:**

  Create a sense of familiarity and trust with your audience.

- **Use social media to showcase your corporate social responsibility and sustainability efforts:**

  Create a sense of purpose and meaning that inspires loyalty and drives business results.

- **Engage with your audience:**

  Create a deeper connection with your followers and increase their trust in your brand.

- **Offer exclusive promotions, deals, and discounts:**

  Increase their loyalty and drive business results.

- **Create compelling and engaging content:**

  Add value to your audience's lives with content that resonates with them.

· · · · · · · ● · · · · · · · · · · ·

chapter 7 cheat sheet

Chapter 7 was all about using storytelling in content marketing to create compelling and engaging content that resonates with your audience. By using storytelling to create content that adds value and entertains, you can drive business results.

To apply the lessons learned in this chapter, implement the following action plan:

- **Align with your target audience's interests and emotions:**

  Use these elements to create a content strategy that resonates with your audience.

- **Create a variety of content formats:**

  Content creation can include blog posts, videos, infographics, and social media posts, that feature customer testimonials, case studies, behind-the-scenes looks, and product demos to showcase the value of your products and services.

- **Create a consistent narrative across all of your content:**

  This will help to build a deeper connection with your audience and increase brand recall.

- **Make your content easily shareable:**

  This will help to increase visibility and reach new audiences.

- **Track the performance of your content:**

  Use this information to refine your content strategy and improve the effectiveness of your storytelling.

- **Invest in high-quality visuals:**

  Enhance your stories and make them more engaging.

- **Leverage the power of social media:**

  Use platforms like Instagram and Facebook to share behind-the-scenes looks, customer testimonials, and other storytelling content to build a deeper connection with your audience.

- **Encourage your audience to share their own stories:**

  Use this user-generated content to create a sense of community and build trust with your audience.

- **Communicate your brand's mission, values, and corporate social responsibility efforts:**

  This will help to create a sense of purpose and meaning that resonates with your audience and drives business results.

chapter 8 cheat sheet

In Chapter 8, we talked about how to use storytelling to connect with customers on an emotional level and create a sense of purpose and meaning. By using storytelling to tap into the emotions of your audience, you can create meaningful connections and drive business results.

To apply the lessons learned in this chapter, implement the following action plan:

- **Conduct market research:**

  Gather information on how your brand is perceived and what emotions it evokes.

- **Tap into the emotions of your audience:**

  Use storytelling to showcase how your brand or products have positively impacted the lives of your customers. Share customer testimonials, success stories, and case studies.

- **Communicate the values and mission of your brand:**

  Share the story of how your brand came to be and the purpose behind it. Use storytelling to create a sense of purpose and meaning that resonates with your audience.

- **Use storytelling in all aspects of your marketing:**

  Include storytelling in your website, social media, email marketing, and other marketing materials.

- **Showcase your brand's commitment to causes:**

  Use storytelling to communicate your corporate social responsibility and sustainability efforts.

- **Create a consistent brand voice and message:**

  Use storytelling to create a sense of familiarity and trust with your audience.

- **Highlight the emotional impact of your products and services:**

  Use storytelling to create a deeper connection with your customers and make them feel like they are part of your brand's story.

- **Improve customer engagement:**

  Use storytelling to make your customers feel like they are a part of your brand's journey. Encourage them to share their own stories and experiences with your brand.

- **Measure the success of your storytelling efforts:**

  Use analytics and metrics to track the effectiveness of your storytelling efforts and make adjustments as needed.

· · · · · · · · · ● · · · · · · · · · · ·

chapter 9 cheat sheet

Chapter 9 focused on building trust and credibility with storytelling. By crafting authentic and engaging stories that showcase your products and services, you can create a sense of purpose and meaning that inspires loyalty and drives business results.

To apply the lessons learned in this chapter, implement the following action plan:

- **Craft authentic and engaging stories:**

  Use real-life examples and customer testimonials to make your stories relatable and credible.

- **Communicate the care and expertise that goes into creating your products and services:**

  Share stories about your rigorous testing and quality control processes, the rare and powerful ingredients you use, and the positive impact your products have on people's lives.

- **Create a sense of purpose and meaning:**

  Share stories that evoke feelings of trust, reliability, and positivity.

- **Communicate your corporate social responsibility and sustainability efforts:**

  Share stories about your commitment to social and environmental causes and how your products and services contribute to making the world a better place.

- **Leverage the power of social media:**

  Use storytelling to create meaningful connections and drive business results by creating compelling and engaging content that resonates with your audience.

- **Create compelling and engaging content:**

  Use storytelling to create content that adds value and entertains.

- **Maintain consistency in your storytelling:**

  This will help create a sense of familiarity and trust with your audience.

- **Encourage customers to share their own stories:**

  Share these stories on your website, social media channels, and other marketing materials to create a sense of trust and credibility with your audience.

······●······

chapter 10 cheat sheet

Finally, in Chapter 10, we learned about using storytelling to communicate your corporate social responsibility and sustainability efforts. By using storytelling to showcase your commitment to social and environmental causes, you can create a sense of purpose and meaning that inspires loyalty and drives business results.

To apply the lessons learned in this chapter, implement the following action plan:

- **Identify causes that align with your brand:**

  Examples could include supporting local communities, reducing carbon emissions, or promoting sustainable practices.

- **Showcase your commitment to these causes:**

  Highlight actions your brand is taking to make a positive impact. These stories can take the form of written content, video, or images, and should highlight the specific actions your brand is taking and the positive impact they are having.

- **Share these stories online:**

  Increase awareness and engagement with your audience. Use storytelling to create a sense of purpose and meaning that resonates with your audience, and inspire them to take action and support your brand.

- **Create a sense of trust and credibility with your audience:**

  Share the specific actions you are taking to support these causes. Also, use storytelling to showcase the positive impact these actions are having on the communities and causes you are supporting.

- **Create a sense of purpose and meaning:**

  Inspire loyalty and drive business results by highlighting the positive impact your brand is having in the world.

- **Create a consistent narrative:**

  Be transparent and authentic in your messaging. This will help to build trust and credibility with your audience, and inspire them to take action and support your brand.

Final Thoughts

As you continue to grow and evolve your brand, remember to keep storytelling at the forefront of your marketing efforts. Use it to connect with your audience on an emotional level, differentiate your brand, and build trust and credibility. Keep experimenting and finding new ways to tell your brand's story, and always be open to learning and growing as a brand.

Oh, and do me a favour. Send me an email. I'm always looking for new and interesting brand stories to share, and I'd love to hear about yours.

Now go out there and use the power of storytelling to stay forever resilient!

About The Author

· · · · · · ● · · · · · · · ·

Mahfuz Chowdhury is a national award-winning brand strategist, storyteller, keynote speaker, and podcast host. Mahfuz regularly helps brands, leaders, and changemakers amplify their brand voice and inspire others through high-impact stories. Mahfuz is also the host of the Modern Mindset podcast, a show where he shares open thoughts on the subject of personal branding and self-development.

He is also the author of Project Reinvention, a book where he shares how he overcame obstacles and reinvented himself in the marketing industry.

· · · · · · ● · · · · · · · ·

Connect with Mahfuz

Website: mahfuzchowdhury.com

Email: mahfuz@engagethroughstories.com

Instagram: @mahfuzc

LinkedIn: /in/mahfuzchowdhury/

References

1. S. Barker, *How to Create High-Converting Content*.
    Content Marketing Institute, 2021.
    https://contentmarketinginstitute.com/

2. C. De Balanzó & N. S. Abad, *Memory: Much More Than Recall.*
    Neuromarketing Science and Business Association, n.d.
    https://www.nmsba.com/

3. C. Da Costa, *3 Reasons Why Brand Storytelling Is The Future Of Marketing*.
    Forbes, 2019.
    https://www.forbes.com/sites/celinnedacosta/

4. R. Carliner, *5 Things Hollywood Taught Me About Being An Entrepreneur*.
    Forbes, 2018.
    https://www.forbes.com/sites/forbeslacouncil/

5. J. Aaker, *Harnessing the Power of Stories*.
    Stanford University, 2019.
    https://womensleadership.stanford.edu/

6. Unknown, *What is Story-Based Strategy?*
    Center for Story-Based Strategy, 2019
    https://www.storybasedstrategy.org/

7. J. Wertz, *How To Scale Personalization Online*.
    Forbes, 2021.
    https://www.forbes.com/sites/jiawertz

8. Unknown, *The Psychology of Sharing: Why Do People Share Online?*
    New York Times, 2011
    http://text-ex-machina.co.uk/blog/new-york-times-study.html

9. Unknown, *How Social Media Impacts Brand Marketing.*
    Nielsen, 2011.
    https://www.nielsen.com/

10. Greater Good Magazine, Various.
    University of California, 2020.
    https://greatergood.berkeley.edu/

11. Unknown, *72% Of U.S. Consumers Want Brands To Reflect Their Values.*
    Retail TouchPoints, 2020.
    https://www.retailtouchpoints.com/

12. N. Senyard, *The Power Of Storytelling To Drive Your Point Home*.
    Forbes, 2022
    https://www.forbes.com/sites/forbesagencycouncil/

13. Unknown, *Brand Storytelling: Why Words Matter as Much as Design*.
    Content Marketing Institute. (2012).
    https://contentmarketinginstitute.com/

14. J. Hall, *Why Brand Credibility Is Essential In Creating An Identity.*
    Forbes, 2021
    https://www.forbes.com/sites/johnhall/

15. V. Afshar, *50 Important Customer Experience Stats for Business Leaders*.
    Huffington Post, 2017.
    https://www.huffpost.com/

16. J. Muthoni, *How Brands Can Employ Visual Storytelling To Engage Target Audiences.*
    Forbes, 2021
    https://www.forbes.com/sites/forbesagencycouncil/

17. K. Wagner, *81% of Small and Medium-Sized Businesses Use Social Media*.
    Mashable, 2014.
    https://mashable.com/archive/linkedin-social-media-study

18. Unknown, *2022 State Of B2B Marketing Technology.*
    Demand Gen Report, 2022.
    https://www.demandgenreport.com/

19. B. J. Bronnenberg, J. Dubé & S. Moorthy, *The Economics of Brands and Branding. Social Science Research Network*. 2018.
    https://papers.ssrn.com/sol3/papers.cfm?abstract_id=3244180

20. Unknown, *7 Things B2B Content Marketers Need in 2023.*
    Content Marketing Institute, 2022.
    https://contentmarketinginstitute.com/

21. A. McKinnon, *4 Tips For Authentic Branded Content.*
    Nielsen, 2021.
    https://www.nielsen.com/

22. J. Friedman, *How to Evolve Your Storytelling for Better Engagement and Conversion*.
    Contently, 2022.
    https://contently.com/

23. Unknown, *The 10 Most Socially Responsible Brands to Model.*
    Grow Ensemble, 2022.
    https://growensemble.com/